Martin A. M. Gansinger

Radical religious thought in Black popular music

Five Percenters and Bobo Shanti in Rap and Reggae

Anchor Academic
Publishing

Gansinger, Martin A. M.: Radical religious thought in Black popular music.
Five Percenters and Bobo Shanti in Rap and Reggae, Hamburg, Anchor Academic
Publishing 2017

Buch-ISBN: 978-3-96067-198-5
PDF-eBook-ISBN: 978-3-96067-698-0
Druck/Herstellung: Anchor Academic Publishing, Hamburg, 2017
Covermotiv: © pixabay.de

Bibliografische Information der Deutschen Nationalbibliothek:
Die Deutsche Nationalbibliothek verzeichnet diese Publikation in der Deutschen
Nationalbibliografie; detaillierte bibliografische Daten sind im Internet über
http://dnb.d-nb.de abrufbar.

Bibliographical Information of the German National Library:
The German National Library lists this publication in the German National Bibliography.
Detailed bibliographic data can be found at: http://dnb.d-nb.de

All rights reserved. This publication may not be reproduced, stored in a retrieval system
or transmitted, in any form or by any means, electronic, mechanical, photocopying,
recording or otherwise, without the prior permission of the publishers.

Das Werk einschließlich aller seiner Teile ist urheberrechtlich geschützt. Jede Verwertung
außerhalb der Grenzen des Urheberrechtsgesetzes ist ohne Zustimmung des Verlages
unzulässig und strafbar. Dies gilt insbesondere für Vervielfältigungen, Übersetzungen,
Mikroverfilmungen und die Einspeicherung und Bearbeitung in elektronischen Systemen.

Die Wiedergabe von Gebrauchsnamen, Handelsnamen, Warenbezeichnungen usw. in
diesem Werk berechtigt auch ohne besondere Kennzeichnung nicht zu der Annahme,
dass solche Namen im Sinne der Warenzeichen- und Markenschutz-Gesetzgebung als frei
zu betrachten wären und daher von jedermann benutzt werden dürften.

Die Informationen in diesem Werk wurden mit Sorgfalt erarbeitet. Dennoch können
Fehler nicht vollständig ausgeschlossen werden und die Diplomica Verlag GmbH, die
Autoren oder Übersetzer übernehmen keine juristische Verantwortung oder irgendeine
Haftung für evtl. verbliebene fehlerhafte Angaben und deren Folgen.

Alle Rechte vorbehalten

© Anchor Academic Publishing, Imprint der Diplomica Verlag GmbH
Hermannstal 119k, 22119 Hamburg
http://www.diplomica-verlag.de, Hamburg 2017
Printed in Germany

Dedicated to Loubna and Ahmed-Nouri

Acknowledgments

I would like to thank Barbara Makeda Blake-Hannah for her support and encouragement during the realization of this project, big up di Empress! Further thanks go to Black Rasta and Big Youth in Kokrobite; Ras Kweku and DJ Isaac in Cape Coast; Paul in Kumasi; Louis Wonder and Las Vegas at the Art Center as well as Abdou, Tanko and Picolo in Accra; the Honorable Priest Ferdinand and the Honorable Priest Henry in Koforidua/New Tafo; Prof. John Collins at the University of Ghana/Accra; my office mate Dr. Ayman Kole for enduring weeks of repeated listening to 'sweet' Jamaican music.

Table of Content

Introduction	9
Contextual Framework	11
Research Interest and Methodology	17
The influence of religion on Black popular music from a historical perspective	23
From Bobo Hill to Billboard Charts: Traces of Bobo Shanti identity and doctrine in Jamaican popular music	27
Expressed doctrine and ideology among Bobo Shanti artists: Similarities and differences in regard to Five Percenter Rap	34
A) Re-interpretation of terminology and the establishment of counterknowledge: *Burning you with Words, Power and Sound*	34
B) Dogmatic perceptions and symbolism: *When the Two Sevens Clash*	40
C) Attitude towards other religious groups and ethnic discrimination: *Fire Pon Rome*	45
D) Visibility and declared affiliation of artists	59
E) Moral superiority, dietary approach and attitude towards drugs	71
F) Attitude towards gender and homosexuality	82
From Mecca to Zion, from Priest to God: Lost children and hybrid identities	97
Outlook and discussion: *What's today's mathematics – fyah still ah bun?*	101
Conclusion	110
References	118
Discography	156

About the author

Dr. Martin Abdel Matin Gansinger (born 1979 in Austria) studied Communication Science and Political Science at the University of Vienna and passed both with distinction. His Master's thesis discusses recursive patterns of cultural, social, and political resistance in various forms of Black American musical expression and the potential of Hip Hop as an alternative communication-structure for the compensation of dysfunctional representation through mainstream-media. He furthermore analyzed the conditions of communication and interaction in regard to the practice of collective improvisation as a musical method and its correspondence to the concept of the Ideal Speech Situation as introduced by Habermas – as well as its efficiency in the context of Intercultural Communication – to attain a Doctor's degree in Communication Science. Next to being an editor and journalist for *jazzzeit* magazine and Vienna-based radio station orange 94.0 from 2005-2009 he has been working as a PR-coordinator for the internationally awarded, independent label JazzWerkstatt Records. Martin Abdel Matin Gansinger conducted several long-term field studies abroad, receiving financial funding through the University of Vienna's research scholarship. He spent a year in Ghana in coordination with the Vienna Institue for Development and Cooperation and Prof. John Collins from the University of Ghana/Accra, researching Intercultural Communication processes in the context of transfusional West African music styles – including an extended stay at the local compound of the Jamaica-based Bobo Shanti Mansion, one of the strictest subdivisions of the Rastafarian faith, and allowance to their communal Nyahbinghi ceremonies. Further field research aiming at extemporaneous communication techniques and its use in traditional knowledge systems has been done in Fez/Morocco and the convent of the Naqshbandi Sufi order in Lefke/Cyprus where he is working and residing since 2009. He is currently holding the position of an Assistant Professor at the Faculty of Communication at Girne American University, teaching Undergraduate-, Master-, and PhD-classes as well as appointed Head of Department of Radio, TV & Cinema. In 2017, Martin A. M. Gansinger initiated *immediate. Currents in Communication, Culture and Philosophy.*

Introduction

Popular music has always drawn part of its attracting powers from referring to religiously connotated sources, obscure movements or charismatic characters in content and symbolism (Till, 2010). One only needs to think about The Beatles' association with Indian gurus, Led Zeppelin's fascination with occultist Aleister Crowley, countless Rock bands' claimed affiliation with the Church of Satan or Rap-millionaire Jay-Z's lucrative play with Illuminati symbolism (Gosa, 2011, p. 8). Providing the listener with seemingly meaningful context beyond the plain musical content seems to help to sell that extra bunch of records.

While in a lot of cases, this displayed affiliation stays mainly on the surface of things and seems to serve simple marketing agendas, some artists openly commit themselves – or even fully dedicate their artistic output – to the cause of certain quasi-religious movements. If the Wu-Tang Clan as one of the most influential Rap groups of the 1990s – at the peak of their popularity, and probably the one of Hip Hop as a genre as well – decided to fill the seven minutes of the first track (Wu-Tang Clan, 1997a) on their highly anticipated new album with a preacher-style sermon performed by Five Percenter ideologist Popa Wu (Killmann, 2014), it can be considered a fundamental statement, underlining the crucial commitment of the artists towards its primary ideological influence.

What might be in coherence with the character of the Five Percent Nation as a missionary movement – employing newspapers and websites or street academy activities (Knight, 2013, p. 96) – comes across a lot more ambivalent in the case of Reggae/Dancehall artists like Sizzla Kalonji, Capleton or Lutan Fyah – who openly demonstrate their affiliation with the Bobo Shanti Order, a rather reclusive branch of the Rastafarian faith, organized around strict communal services (Barnett, 2002, p. 58) and quite clear in its rejective stance towards Reggae music (Kamimoto, 2015, p. 47).

However, one of the main questions that has to be asked is concerning the possible reasons for the fact that two highly commercially successful, globally relevant and influential musical styles of the last decades (Savishinsky, 1994a; Mitchell, 2001; Alim, Ibrahim, & Pennycook, 2008) being tied to rather obscure mythologies of somehow radical religious character that affiliated artists pledge open allegiance to. Are these ideologies simply being instrumentalized by musicians looking for increased attention by adding some outstanding attitude and identity on a competitive market – or are they in turn being used and exploited for promotional purposes? In any case, it is nothing else but astonishing that a considerable audience of listeners would happily vibe to rather harsh and violent musical enforcements of Mosaic law, delivered by preachy, self-styled prophets – or even more obscure, Islam-inspired Black supremacy conceptions, circulating around the idea that the creation of the Caucasian race is resulting from an evil experiment of a mad scientist (Smith, 1998, p. 539).

Contextual Framework

The inflationary use of the term 'radical' by news media outlets within the last few years – and its tendency of it being attached to Islamic routine and common practice such as the wearing of headscarfs, prayer hats, beards, traditional clothes or the simple act of prayer itself as indications for extremist thought and behavior – is asking for a closer consideration about the connotation of the word in the context of this discussion. Here, unlike the more hysterical and polarizing depictions in news media, the term is used neither as a positive nor as a negative evaluation but simply refers to the relatively strict adherence to rather restrictive concepts and beliefs. Therefore, it applies to the strong emphasis of the Bobo Shanti Rasta Mansion on the Old Testament and a strict schedule of commune-oriented practices such as the honoring of the Sabbath or regular fasting – which clearly sets it apart from more moderate and less regulative Rastafarian branches like the Twelve Tribes of Israel (Rubenstein & Suarez, 1994; Chevannes, 1994, p. 171).

In case of the Five Percent Nation – founded 1964 in Harlem – the radical aspect is given by a crude creation mythology based on reversed racism that is somehow shared with other Black nationalist movements (Isma'ilis, 2014; McCloud, 2014) such as the Nation of Islam (Essien-Udom, 1962; Tinaz, 1996; Tinaz, 2000; Tinaz, 2001; Bowen, 2013) or the Nuwaubian Nation (Bailey, 2006; Palmer, 2010; Finley, Guillory, & Page, Jr., 2014) but certainly sets it apart from orthodox Islam (Swedenburg, 1996, p. 2; Knight, 2013, p. 91). One just needs to consider that the body of its founder – Clarence 13X Smith, a former member of the Nation of Islam, referred to by his followers as *Father Allah* – was cremated after his assassination in 1969 (Knight, 2013), while orthodox Islam strictly requires the corpse to be buried in the soil. Similarly, despite considerable references to Biblical texts – especially the *Psalms of David* in the Old Testament (Murrell, 2000) – and adherence to orthodox rites, Semaj (2013, p. 107) pointed to *the Rasta tradition of 'let the dead bury their dead'* and *the absence of rites of passage* as (o)*ne major sign in the stagnation of the Rasta culture* (p. 106), with funerals for dead Rastas *being facilitated at the church of their parents or the one they had abandoned when they answered the calling of Rastafari* (p. 107). He furthermore stressed the absence of either original or religious rituals for marriage, *which is either by common-law unions, the laws of the state (Babylon) or a series of casual, undefined relationships* (p. 106), as well as missing ceremonies for birth and the naming of children.

Although the Bobo Shanti Order – also known as Bobo Ashanti or the Ethiopian African Black International Congress Church of Salvation (EABIC), founded 1958 in Kingston by Prince Emmanuel Charles Edwards, today referred to as King Emmanuel I or *Dada* by his followers – is strongly based on religious concepts and traditions, the Five Percent Nation as well as the Rastafari ideology as a whole tend to stick to a self-definition that puts more emphasis on cultural or ethnical aspects and occasionally show efforts to distance themselves from institutionalized religion (Washington, 2014, p. 86; Gibbs, 2003, p. 91). Nevertheless, they might still be classified as quasi-religious movements – with even less orthodox Rasta denominations than the Bobo Shanti being based on strict adherence to varying divine conceptions (Hannah, 1981; Rubenstein & Suarez, 1994; Barnett, 2005) or at least attributing a strong inherent spiritual aspect to their lifestyle and belief system (Huhtala, 2015) by frequently using the term 'faith' to describe it (Taylor, 2005). As pointed out by Zips (2006, p. 135), (t)*he Bobo Ashanti state and church are not separated which is demonstrated by the double functions of the political decision makers as priests of the Melchizedec Righteous Kingdom*. On the other hand, the Nation of Islam has been attested state-religious character by Essien-Udom (1962) and the Five Percenters conception of each (Black) man being God was defined as a *highly innovative and idiosyncratic religious expression* (Gibbs, 2003, p. 91). In coherence with this individual approach of self-realization, his acknowledgment of strong gnostic influences in Five Percenter teachings led Knight (2013, p. 232) to categorize it as *some sort of indigenous African American Sufism*, in accordance with O'Connor (1998). Nevertheless, Knight also suggested a relativation of that very claim at the same time, noting that Clarence 13X Smith had clearly positioned himself as anti-religion – as contrary to the conception of classical Sufism (Knight, 2013, p. 232):

> *It is easy to imagine parallels with medieval saints such as Ibn-al-Arabi, who saw man as reflecting the divine, or al-Hallaj, who famously called himself by one of Allah's 99 Names (*al-Haqq*, the 'Truth'). While not always off the mark, it's a naive assumption that Five Percenters approach 'God' with mysticism. Sufi themes of divine union or Manifesting God's Attributes represent a closeness to the* mystery god *whose existence is denied in the 120.*

In this context it is necessary to note that *the 120* at the end of the above quote refers to *the 120 degrees*, the core teachings of the Five Percenters. Even though more based on esoteric than exoteric principles (Gray, 2014), both groups classify as offsprings from a broader religiously connotated ideology and while the Five Percent Nation tends to be less regulated, more moderate and individually-oriented in reference to the Nation of Islam as its core inspiration, it still classifies as being termed as radical and extremist in more than one aspect. Media comparisons of Five Percenters to the Hitler Youth in the 1960s (Knight, 2013, p. 122) and an infamous appearance of the Wu-Tang Clan on the Arsenio Hall Show in 1994 with Ol' Dirty Bastard – Five Percenter name Unique Aason Allah (Knight, 2013, p. 184) – provocatively shouting *'the Black Man is God!'* (2013, p. 182) in the face of a mainstream American audience might serve as evidence for the widespread consideration of the group as radical in the public eye. The Bobo Shanti on their behalf have been termed as *Reggae Mullahs* or *Jamaican Taliban* by critics and other artists (Midnite, 2001; DancehalDopeBoi, 2013) who put the religion-based, judgmental views and rigid lifestyle in context with the general attitude of Islamic fundamentalists. Another case of portraying the Five Percent Nation as a sort of hidden *fifth column,* comprised of radical and militant Islamists, could be observed at the occasion of the attempt to link the Washington sniper-shootings of 2002 to the direct influence of affiliated artists like Wu-Tang's Method Man or Killarmy (Swedenburg, 2002; Aidi, 2004; Knight, 2013, p. 185; Hassell, 2015). For the purpose of this discussion the name *Five Percent Nation* will be used to address the group, since the later on established and simultaneously employed *Nation of the Gods and Earths* does not seem to be fully accepted in the somewhat fragmented movement (Knight, 2013, p. 200).

In regard to a conceptual perspective, the following discussion draws heavily from a comparative analysis of the Nation of Islam and the Rastafari philosophy (Barnett, 2006), which can be considered as the respective roots from which the Five Percenters and the Bobo Shanti emerged. Soumahoro (2007) provided a less complex approach of portraying shared elements of Rastafarianism and the Nation of Islam that demonstrates their attempt to challenge Christianity as the theological reference system for the identified oppressive power structures they claim to oppose. Due to a formative and consistent impact on Hip Hop as the most influential cultural movement in terms of music production, aesthetics, fashion, and rentability throughout the last decades, quite considerable attention is given to the Five Percenters from a scholarly perspective.

Aptly placed in the *Journal of Gang Research*, Corbiscello's (1998) slightly judgmental approach focused mainly on controversial aspects of crime- and race-related matters throughout the history of the group, with brief captures of major personalities, symbolism and doctrine. O'Connor (2006) provided an insightful account on theological aspects of the Five Percenters and its status as a kind of alternative religion emerging out of the Islamic African-American community but does not cover its ties to Hip Hop in detail. Swedenburg (1996) authored one of the first attempts that presented samples of doctrine reflected in lyrics of affiliated artists and explored the application of Middle Eastern Islamic culture as an African-American tool for cultural resistance in Islamic Rap. A similar angle has been chosen by Aidi (2004) and Alim (2006), who portrayed different layers of Islamic influence on US-Hip Hop, from Sunni Islam to the Nation of Islam and Five Percenters.

Miyakawa's (2005) extensive and detailed attempt to analyze the reflection of Five Percenters in Hip Hop culture from a musicologist's point of view – aiming at traceable references in lyrical content, rhythmical patterns, symbolism in artwork and even hidden numerology in the order the tracks are assembled for an album – has been criticized by Knight (2013, p. 227) for not considering a field research approach in order to capture first-hand views of the movement. Assuming that they would not tolerate whites among their ranks – as has been the case with the Nation of Islam (p. 229) –, Miyakawa did not consider a personal inquiry to approach the group directly. Knight's own work benefited from extensive participant observation among the Five Percenters but touches rather briefly on the various representations of the ideology in Hip Hop – although he provided considerable space to an extensive analysis of Rakim's (Rakim, 1997) *Mystery (Who Is God?)*, which he termed *a masterpiece of both hip-hop artistry and NGE metaphysics* (Knight, 2013, p. 180).

However, due to the fact that the wide-scale, direct and consistent influence of Five Percenter ideology on Rap music and Hip Hop culture has already been sufficiently illustrated by Miyakawa's work, the purpose of this discussion will mainly consist of accentuating a similar stringent and cohesive influence of Bobo Shanti doctrine in the area of Jamaican music, specifically Dancehall-Reggae. Chevannes (1977), Owens (1977) and Niiah (2005) provided insightful reviews on literature that is based on more general accounts of Rastafarian Studies. The latter suggested a divison between early journalistic material throughout the 1930s, *academic expositions* (2005, p.12) since the 1950s (Simpson, 1955; Smith, Augier, & Nettleford, 1967; Kitzinger, 1969; Edmonds, 2002; Zips, 2006) – *reflecting outsider North Atlantic impressions to the local sensitivity* (Niiah, 2005, p. 12) – and *testimonial/autobiographical* (p. 12.) material, provided by members of the group itself (Dizzy, 1967; Hannah, 1981; Mack, 1999).

Pollard (1982) and Slade (2013) are among those who looked at the extended framework of *Dread Talk* that is frequently being employed by Jamaican Reggae artists, with the former investigating its social and historical context and the latter focusing on morphological aspects and inherent conceptual meanings of cultural resistance. While Simpson (1985) had looked at legal and political aspects in regard to the religious dimension of the Rastafarian belief, Waters (1985) presented one of the first attempts to link its theological core with the political message of Reggae music. An even more helpful amount of literature – considering the specific scope of this discussion – has been provided by Zips (2003; 2006; 2011; 2015), who offered numerous accounts based on ethnographic research and transnational law in regard to claims of repatriation and reparation, which he deemed strongly enforced and supported by the global visibility of Dancehall-Reggae artists affiliated with the Bobo Shanti Rasta Mansion.

Substantial ethnographic information on dogmatic aspects, habitual behavior and structural organization of the Bobo Shanti Order has been presented by Chevannes (1994), White (2007; 2012) and Tanis (2010). Kamimoto (2015) furthermore addressed the influence of Reggae music on the economic activities of the Order by focusing on the shift of occupational patterns among the Bobo community in Bull Bay, Jamaica, from traditional, handicraft-oriented means of income towards participation in activities related to the music industry – as a direct consequence of the growing popularity of Bobo Shanti artists. By clearly portraying the ongoing conflict between the sacred and the secular, the traditional and the innovation, the righteous occupation and the fast money, Kamimoto managed to demonstrate the ambivalent – but nevertheless undisputable strong – impact of musicians affiliated with the Order on the rather reclusive community. Together with Pereira (1998), who had already pointed out the considerable religious connotations inherent to Roots Reggae that rather surprisingly surfaced and flooded the more secular Dancehall genre from the mid-1990s on, the aforementioned contributions helped to articulate the approach of this discussion, which shall be layed out in detail throughout the following part.

Research Interest and Methodology

The main interest here will be to allow conclusions about whether or not the representation of Bobo Shanti ideology in Jamaican Dancehall-Reggae is corresponding with the attested influence of the Five Percent Nation on US-Hip Hop in degree and directional patterns. It is intended to shed light on the question of how Bobo Shanti artists incorporate considerable elements of religious identity in their creative output as well as pointing out similarities and differences between Five Percenter conceptions as presented in US-Hip Hop and Bobo Shanti doctrine in Jamaican Dancehall-Reggae. However, it is important to note that Five Percenter officials willingly cooperate with affiliated artists to spread the message and publicly appear in videos (Knight, 2013, p. 179), while in the case of the Bobo Shanti it appears to be more of a one-directional flow, in which artists praise and promote the doctrine without official involvement of the Order and explicit approval of its representatives (Kamimoto, 2015). As a central time frame for the discussion, the two decades around the millenial turn have been decided upon, due to the unquestionable peak of popularity and influence of central artists affiliated with the two ideologies around that time. Whether or not there might be a common pattern, indicating a correspondance with generally increased interest in religion and spirituality in the wave of endtime scenarios around the Y2K hype being reflected in popular culture (Schaefer, 2004; Bendle, 2005) is a question that exceeds the limits of this discussion, however. Furthermore, more recent examples will be taken into consideration in order to discuss patterns of continuity and change.

The methodological approach of the following discussion is mainly based on a descriptive case study (Simons, 1980; Yin, 1984; Stake, 1995), with the core substance being Jamaican Dancehall-Reggae performed by artists affiliated with the Bobo Shanti Rasta Order. Following the theoretical conception of Yin (1984), multiple sources of evidence – from lyrical and visual primary sources to ethnographic evidence collected in a field research situation – will be considered to increase internal validity. As for external validity, next to the consideration of existing literature as secondary sources of evidence, the design of a cross-case study has been chosen, in which the core substance content will be contrasted with findings concerning the influence of Five Percenter ideology on US-Hip Hop. Miyakawa's approach to analyze how lyrics reveal the inner workings of the Five Percenter theology (2005, p. 41) and her conception of artists as authoratative teachers that offer personal testimonials by quoting, paraphrasing and interpreting the movements doctrine (p. 42) can be applied in a similar way to the Bobo Shanti Rasta Mansion and its affiliated artists.

Therefore, not unlike Miyakawa's work , next to building on existing literature, a multi-layered analysis using Fairclough's model of Critical Discourse Analysis (1992) – considering textual, discoursive, and social practices – has been taken into consideration. Hence, non-verbal communication such as dress code and overall appearance, semiotic conceptions and considerations, as well as demonstrated coherence between expressed views and attitudes in song titles and lyrical content are expected to provide information about corresponding patterns of ideological influence and basic doctrine. The references taken into consideration will solely be limited to indications that carry religious connotations related to the Bobo Shanti doctrine, therefore more general expressions dealing with common patterns of the Rastafarian agenda – such as repatriation or socio-political criticism – will not be considered. Findings will be contrasted with corresponding samples of Five Percenter artists in order to define potential differences and similarities. In reference to the expressed confrontational stance of Rastafari- and Black Power-movements alike, Singh (2004) identified the use of religion, dress, hair, drugs and music as central elements in their pursuence of *an ideal concept of reality in which social change and social action were manifested in more symbolic rather than concrete forms* (p. 32). Partly based on these criterias, the following factors have been determined to operationalize the subject matter, identify patterns of influence and provide defined categories for discussion:

A) Re-interpretation of terminology and the establishment of counterknowledge: inclusion of coded language derived from ideological vocabulary and concepts

B) Dogmatic perceptions and symbolism: references to basic concepts of the respective religious doctrine in verbal and visual representations

C) Attitude towards other religious groups and ethnic discrimination: consideration of exclusive and inclusive tendencies in regard to orthodox religion and comparable competitive branches as well as issues of ethnicity and racism reflecting characteristic practices among the respective group

D) Visibility and declared affiliation of artists: demonstrative gestures of allegiance in the form of dress code, habitual behavior or verbal declaration, juxtaposed with data that sheds light on the actual consideration of artists among the respective group

E) Moral superiority, dietary approach and attitude towards drugs: verbal claims of moral superiority based on the respective group's regulations in regard to diet and drugs

F) Attitude towards gender and homosexuality: correspondance between doctrinal perceptions of gender issues and expressed views in conduct and articulation

Due to their distinctive consistency and visibility in terms of Bobo-affiliation – as well as being among the most popular and critically acclaimed artists associated with the Order – the cited references will to a large degree be comprised of examples from the creative output of Sizzla, Capleton and Lutan Fyah (recipient of the International Reggae and World Music Award for Spiritual Service Through Music in 2009 – Roberts, 2011). The corresponding patterns they are compared to mainly stem from the

Rap groups Brand Nubian – *a virtual missionary wing for the Nation of the Gods and Earths* (Knight, 2013, p. 179) – and Wu-Tang Clan as some of the most active and visible musical ambassadors of the Five Percent Nation, heavily referenced by Miyakawa (2005) as well.

While the strictly defined and canonized Five Percenter lessons – being documented and memorized word for word in *the 120*, as mentioned earlier – provided a precise frame of reference for the directly quoted or paraphrased mentionings found in the output of affiliated artists, the situation is somewhat different in the context of the Bobo Shanti teachings, that are more corresponding to informal initiations, aquired during a personal training period. Further difficulties occur from the fact that Bobo doctrine presents itself more intermingled with general Rastafarian philosophy – in terms of sharing the same vocabulary, concepts and behavioral patterns – than the more distinctive and defined Five Percenters, who clearly set themselves apart from orthodox Islam as well as other Black Muslim movements. However, Bobos would stand out more in regard to personal appearance, which is asking for a multidimensional approach focusing on more than just the examination of lyrical content. To fill this gap, the discussion incorporates existing literature to juxtapose the selected samples as well as data collected in the course of an ethnographic field research conducted at the Bobo Shanti settlement in Koforidua/Ghana in 2007, adding information generated from primary sources.

The nine-months field study project in Ghana has been developed and conducted in accordance with the Vienna Institute for Development and Cooperation and was partly financed with research grants provided by the Department for Research Services and International Relations of The University of Vienna. After getting stopped at the gate house of the Bobo compound in Koforidua, the first point that the Honorable Priest Dennis Mills – who made a rather surprising appearance in torn boxer shorts and a worn out Mickey Mouse T-shirt after being interrupted in his sleep by the guardian in charge and therefore presenting a quite sharp contrast to the dignified robes and attire he usually can be seen with on pictures (Zips & Kämpfer, 2001; Zips, 2005) – tried to get across in a rather aggravated manner was the fact that life in his entrusted community is far from a *reggae and reefer*-type beach party. Based on strict religious commitment, residents would be expected to agree with regular fasts at least twice a week, a vegan diet, separated genders, scheduled labor duties and participate in daily communal worship ceremonies. In addition, the Honorable Priest Dennis Mills made it clear that the Bobos in Koforidua are extremely concerned about being infiltrated by CIA agents and therefore ask visitors to hand over cameras and phones to the guardian at the entrance gate house, alongside any kind of official documents that are not permitted on the compound due to the community's severe rejection of any type of governmental link to imperialistic, neo-colonial rule.

Due to the rather strict settings on the compound and somehow sceptical attitude of the residing population, an adjustable mix of explorative, qualitative methodological instruments has been applied to collect data. In accordance with suggestions by Atteslander (1995) and Girtler (1984), an explorative, non-structured, active and open qualitative participant observation (Howell, 1973) on an 'observer-as-participant' level of involvement has been chosen to provide flexibility in the field and reduce the risk of ethnocentristically flawed structural frames – combined with non-structured narrative interviews. As a matter of fact, the conditions for the study quite improved after mentioning the name of anthropologist Werner Zips, who immediatly got identified as *the Austrian professor*, due to his previous visits on the compound – which enabled the establishment of a more beneficial research atmosphere and rather cooperative attitutes. However, the role of the researcher has somehow been pre-defined by the Order's general perception that every non-member basically belongs to the *lost children*, that have to be introduced to the teachings of Rastafari and King Emmanuel I – meaning that they are basically willing to pass on informations as part of a moderate missionary effort, once the trainee has accepted to submit to the rules of the community and participates in the prescribed services. Due to the fact that the results mainly serve to counterbalance the findings of the identified and analyzed discoursive elements, the typical method of thick description will not be applied in this case study. The findings will rather be contrasted with the discussion of the defined categories by using thematic analysis that allows the organizing of data according to the respective aspects at hand.

During the period of the stay, the compound – which is located in close proximity to a nearby settlement of villagers – was populated by the Honorable Priests Henry, Ferdinand and Dennis Mills, all of them expatriates from Jamaica sent to Ghana in accordance to the repatriation politics of the Bobo Shanti. Further inhabitants included two Priests in training that displayed the typical behavior of young adepts in spiritual or religious circles by being rather closed and seemingly seeking to chastise themselves, as well as a female member of the Order, kept away from male company during the rather generous amount of twenty-one days a month she is considered impure. Social life in the compound circulates around a big wooden building in its center, referred to as the Holy Tabernacle, where the communal sacred services are held. Priests in training and visitors alike are obliged to start the day at sunrise by turning towards the East, wave the characteristic black, red, and green colored Bobo flags and chant the Biblical verses of the Psalms of David. Trainees furthermore engage in organizational obligations around the compound, that also grows its own fruits and vegetables. Priests are granted a more laid-back lifestyle and are usually focusing on individual meditations over Biblical texts, instructional *reasonings* or short visits to the nearby settlement. On Saturday – the day of the Sabbath – everybody is supposed to abstain from any activity but worship. Communal services in the Holy Tabernacle are scheduled on Friday at 6 p.m. – the beginning of the Sabbath – as well as Saturday noon and evening and inolve the chanting of Psalms and Nyahbinghi drumming.

The influence of religion on Black popular music from a historical perspective

> There is a long relationship between music and religious concerns, the former often serving as a vehicle for the articulation of the latter. What is more, one need not sing explicitely about heaven and hell in order for one's music to wrestle with deeply religious themes.
> (Pinn, 2007, p. 289)

As pointed out in the introductory lines – and in coherence with scholars in Religious and Cultural Studies – the study of music offers *an opportunity to follow the 'flow' of the religious within cultural production* (Pinn, 2007, p. 293) and therefore provides a promising possibility *to better recognize and analyze both religiosity (themes, practices, etc.) and an important cultural ethos marking our new century* (p. 293). Religion and spirituality have always played a certain role in the history of Black musical expressions in the USA (Lovell, 1972; Lincoln, 1974; Spencer, 1991; Spencer, 1995; Floyd, 1996; Harris, 1999; Reed, 2003). The integral function of music as one element among others – dance, vocal articulation, elements of theatralic performances, audience participation – in a bigger, communal cultural experience within the African tradition (Wilson, 1974; Maultsby, 2000) might serve as a possible explanation for that. Once on American soil, their specific status as forced immigrants, systematically alienated from their original culture and identity, made enslaved Africans willingly embrace Christian religion and its promise of an afterlife salvation – as documented in the enthusiastic engagement of Blacks in the performance of church hymns and Gospel music (Williams-Jones, 1975; Boyer, 1979).

Nevertheless, between the lines, the ecstatically invoked hereafter could also be interpreted as the very earthly stretch of land north of the border, where slavery has been abolished and those who made it through the *underground railroad* would find their salvation in the form of freedom, as illustrated by Werner (2006). He furthermore developed a classification system, that divides the various forms of Black musical expression in the USA as being inspired either by a Gospel impulse, a Blues impulse or a Jazz impulse – referring to either optimistic integrationist ideology, rather pessimistic descriptions of the experienced reality of segregation or a creative approach, seeking to question the status quo and developing techniques to transform it into something better. As a consequence, it seems only logical that the Blues has been condemned by Gospel singers as the devil's music (Burnett, 2015; Kornegay, 2013) and later served as an inspiration for more politically oriented criticism, as can be found in Hip Hop, for instance. As pointed out by Aidi (2004, p. 108):

> (J)*ust as racial segregation and Jim Crow laws had its impact on early Jazz and the polished, consens-oriented Soul and Rhythm & Blues of the late 1960s and early 1970s was a product of the civil rights movement, the neoliberalism, urban blight and nihilism, which gave rise to the underclass and produced rap, also gave birth to Islamic hip hop.*

However, from the 1940s on, the Jazz scene turned into a promising hunting ground for various sects based on concepts and beliefs influenced by Islam (Monson, 2000; Turner, 2003; Stowe, 2010). Due to the considerable influence of the missionary – and non-orthodox – Ahmadiyyah movement (O'Connor, 1998; Bayoumi, 2001; Bowen, 2013) and its influence on musicians until the 1960s (Fanusie, 2007; McCloud, 2014), a lot of artists such as Ahmad Jamal, Yusef Lateef, Idries Muhammad and others had adopted Muslim names, sometimes simply to pass as North Africans and avoid racist treatment (Chase, 2010), often inspired by the state-religious claims of the lost-found Nation of Islam (Essien-Udom, 1962; Curtis, 2002; Curtis, 2006; Bowen, 2013). Far from Sunni Islam – which is often referred to as *al-Islam* in the Black community, in order to distinguish it from the various non-orthodox Muslim-inspired movements – the Nation of Islam gained international recognition in the early 1960s under Minister Malcolm X and Cassious Clay/Muhammad Ali as one of its most prominent members. Although Warith Deen Muhammad – the son of founder Elijah Muhammad – attempted to position the movement more close to orthodox Islam during the 1970s, its origins are deeply rooted in the teachings of Noble Drew Ali and his Moorish Science Temple, that also managed to exert a considerable influence on the Jazz scene at some point. As pointed out by Bayoumi and DeCaro (1999), *in the 1960s, jazz became a bridge for Noble Drew Ali's Moorish Science doctrines to reach white hipsters at NYU and Columbia, who then formed their own Moorish Orthodox Church* (Knight, 2013, p. 228). In correspondance with *many younger members of Western societies who were urged to abandon their parents' values and religion* (Poutiainen & Rantakallio, 2016, p. 195), a considerable amount of Jazz musicians *drew their inspiration from Asian religions and philosophy, cosmology, Islam, and Christianity* (p. 195), which is especially true for the Free Jazz/Avantgarde movement (Berkman, 2007; Brown, 2010). Despite striking differences in terms of musical content and direction, similar to *jazz avant-gardists of the 1960s, contemporary Muslim hip-hop artists discuss their relationship to religion through their musical output* (Poutiainen & Rantakallio, 2016, p. 195).

The influence of religion and spirituality on Rap music and Hip Hop culture has been discussed in general (Pinn, 2003; Sanneh & Priest, 1997; Pinn, 2007; Sorett, 2009; Miller, Pinn, & Freeman, 2015) as well as specifically for Islam (Swedenburg, 2001; Floyd-Thomas, 2003; Aidi, 2004; Alim, 2006; Khabeer, 2007; Miah & Kalra, 2008; McMurray, 2007; Aidi, 2013; Washington, 2014). Not even considering the vast amount of artists that are said to be affiliated with the more obscure Nation of Islam (Decker, 1993) and the Five Percent Nation (Ahmed, 2012), Bracey's (2007) claim that *Hip Hop has the potential to spread Islamic thought in much the same way that Reggae spread Rastafarianism* (p. 458) does not seem surprising. The weight of these words gets underlined by the following statement of Savishinsky (1994a, p. 260) – although it might need to be updated in favor of Hip Hop and the Five Percent Nation soon:

> *What is perhaps most interesting and unique about Rastafari is that it may represent the only contemporary socio-religious movement whose diffusion is directly linked to various mediums of transnational popular culture, most notably reggae music.*

The perspective that Reggae music has been the main vehicle to spread the rather obscure Rastafarian conception all over the globe has been argued by scholars throughout the last decades (Savishinsky, 1994a; Pereira, 1998; Walker, 2005; Davis, 2006; Niiah, 2011; Kamimoto, 2015). Therefore, in the following section, the incorporation of Bobo Shanti doctrine as a subdivision of the Rastafarian faith into what used to be secular, Reggae-inspired Jamaican Dancehall music shall be discussed more detailed.

From Bobo Hill to Billboard Charts: Traces of Bobo Shanti identity and doctrine in Jamaican popular music

Similar to the notion of Hip Hop and Rap as an alternative media structure (Gansinger, 2008) or *the black CNN* – as suggested by Chuck D. of Public Enemy (Gold, 1989, p. 16) –, Reggae has been referred to as *the newspaper of Jamaica* (Blatter, 2008, p. 21) for the outspoken social and political commentary of the music in the 1970s that articulated urgent issues related to the still evident structures of colonization in Jamaican society (Miller, 1993) to an audience suffering from high illiteracy rates. Due to a period characterized by economical problems, political tensions (Harrison, 1990) and intensified violence (Harrison, 1988), (i)*n the mid 1980s and through the early '90s, Jamaican music saw a decline in Rastafarian-inspired protest music and an increase in slack music, or songs featuring lyrics of graphic sexuality, gangster life, gunplay, and violence* (Blatter, 2008, p. 24).

As pointed out by Wexler (1994), the internationally successful song *Murderer* (Buju Banton, 1995) by new-born Rasta artist Buju Banton – in which the former Dancehall artist known for typically slack lyrics (Stanley, 2005) strongly condemns gun-inflicted violence by referring to Biblical punishment for violation of the First Commandment – can be seen as a turning point towards a spiritual revival in Jamaican music and society that many people embraced out of disappointment for the inability of politicians to come up with solutions for existing problems. The anti-violence vibe quickly got picked up and commercialized by other artists (Pereira, 1998, p. 34), a broader opposition to slack and violent content – such as *the decision by various members of the Jamaican Federation of Musicians to refuse to provide musical backing for singers of slackness and violence, or a renewed policy of filtering of much of this music by certain of the radio stations and a corresponding promotion of 'spiritual' music* (p. 34) – started to form. Therefore, the conditions of the industry in general started to turn into being beneficial for a re-orientation of attitude and lyrical approach. Similarly, the rhetoric of the Five Percenters started to emerge in Hip Hop during the late 1980s, after a decade of social cuts, crack and violence in the urban areas and little perspectives to fix issues on a political level.

Despite the big number of Dancehall artists discovering their Rasta identity and a wave of Bobo artists such as Capleton, Junior Reid, Anthony B., Sizzla, Jah Mason, Turbulence or Lutan Fyah on the forefront of a morally and religiously charged, internationally commercially successful movement in Jamaican music, it was not the first time that the characteristic tightly wrapped turbans were spotted. One of the first artists to introduce the Bobo dress code in Jamaican popular music has been the Roots Reggae band The Abbyssinians. By wearing the characteristic turban to cover their locks in combination with ceremonial Bobo robes, certain members of The Abbyssinans could be clearly distinguished from other artists by appearance.

However, the lyrical content of the group does not include any direct references to the Order on the other hand. Repatriation hymns such as *Satta Massagana* (The Abbyssinians, 1976) were touching on issues that are by far not exclusive for Bobos and easily fit in with other topics on the noble agenda of the 1970s Conscious Reggae movement that included freedom, equality, justice and liberation for the oppressed, human rights, peace, education or ecological responsibilities.

Despite that, the small island in the Caribbean did not get spared from the overall materialistic ideology of the 1980s, that led to the emerge of the more wordly and aggressive Raggamuffin and Dancehall styles, originated by artists like Count Matchouki, Lord Comic, and King Stitt and mainly popularized by U-Roy in the late 1960s (Hope, 2006, p. 11). Heavily influenced by global popular culture narratives such as Western-, Gangster-, or Samurai-movies (Zips, 2011, p. 143), the movement embraced the re-negotiation of moral values in the rise of capitalism-coined individualism and accentuated the image of the personalized *outlaw* or *bad guy* in

Jamaican music – as represented by artists like Yellowman, Elephant Man, Ninja Man or Shabba Ranks (Hope, 2006). As pointed out by Hope (2009, p. 404):

> (D)ancehall music and culture's movement to the forefront of Jamaican popular music and culture in the early 1980s was perceived by many reggae-purists as the death knell to the Rastafari-infused "conscious reggae" that dominated the cultural landscape of the preceding musical era, a kind of Dark Ages.

However, towards the mid-1990s, several successful Dancehall artists such as the aforementioned Buju Banton – already notorious for his homophobic song *Boom Bye Bye* (Buju Banton, 1992) – converted to the Rastafarian faith. The Bobo Shanti affiliated Capleton emerged from the secular realms of Dancehall as 'The Fireman', *inflamed with the ethos of Rastafari and touting an incendiary brand of dancehall lyrics that was peppered with the teachings and ideas of his Rastafari worldview* (Hope, 2009, p. 405). The following years saw a wave of devoted Bobo Shanti artists such as Anthony B., Sizzla, Jah Mason, Junior Reid, Turbulence, Prophet Benjamin or Lutan Fyah, who would wear the characteristic turbans and joined the *firestarter* on his mission to challenge the capitalist views of the dominating Dancehall scene. Often labeled as *Fire Reggae* (Zips, 2011, p. 151), the newly emerged Rasta deejays (singers) resurrected the outdated Rasta ethos in the more aggressive and contemporary relevant Dancehall sound as the most popular expression of Jamaican music at that time.

In a sharp contrast to the violent, sexualized representations of Dancehall artists like Beenie Man, Vybz Kartell or Bounty Killer, (t)*hey introduced various Rastafari elements to dancehall, including dress, prayer, a clear moral message, and percussion sounds* (Kamimoto, 2015, p. 43), passing as an updated version of typical Rastafarian artists like Fantan Mojah or Mr. Perfect, who would restrict themselves to a contemporary version of Conscious Roots Reggae and consequently abstain from the secular Dancehall style (Hope, 2009, p. 410). As noted by Hope (p. 405), *in Jamaica, the ideological/musical transition of a hardcore dancehall artiste to Rastafari is underscored as a glorious promotion,* that would often be interpreted as a sign that *Jamaica would soon experience a corresponding ideological rebirth and a much-needed social renewal* (2009, p. 407). Therefore, the arrival of the Bobos on the Dancehall scene in the mid-1990s *was perceived as the re-turn of Bob Marley and the death knell for "dutty dancehall" with its explicit and extreme discourses filled with unclothed, erotic female bodies, errect phalluses and unsheathered lyrical guns* (ibid.).

While establishing links with Dancehall as the currently most relevant manifestation of Jamaican popular music, the *obvious cross-fertilization with hardcore patriarchal dancehall culture and patriarchal, incendiary, revolutionary Rastafari in the music of this genre of artistes is epitomized in their "bunning" (burning) of the usual deviants* (Hope, 2009, p. 406) – as illustrated in Anthony B.'s *Fire Pon Rome* (Anthony B., 1996). Although the *burning down of Babylon* has always been part of the Rasta rhetoric, the *pure militancy* (Zips, 2003) of Bobo artists marks a clear evolutionary step in terms of diction and vigorousity compared to the leading Conscious Reggae artists of the 1970s and hints to a direct influence of the Order's radical doctrine and rhetoric, to which it bears clear resemblance to (Chevannes, 1994).

Termed as *hybrid dancehall rasta* (Hope, 2006, p. 14), artists would shock and astonish Conscious Reggae and secular Dancehall audiences alike by blending the specific, as *spiritual, pristine and pure* (Hope, 2009, p. 410) perceived codes of Rastafari philosophy with *notions of sexualized, heterosexual male identity* (p. 410) – as illustrated in Sizzla's *Pump Up* (Sizzla, 2001). This initiated an ongoing identity negotiation between the conflicting requirements and expectations of the clean and humble Rasta lifestyle and the highly competitive, material-centered Dancehall scene (Hope, 2012). Pereira (1998, p. 34) argued that sex may as well simply be considered as a physical, non-conflicting manifestation of a higher spiritual concept of love in the general Rasta philosophy:

> *It is neither that these singers are being inconsistent nor are they being opportunist. Indeed, their reconciliation of sex with spirituality is consistent with a value system that does not dichotomize carnality and spirituality.*

Nevertheless, hardly conform to the more strict and orthodox Bobo Shanti doctrine they claim to follow, Rasta deejays like Sizzla gave way to current phenomenons such as Gangsta Ras, that have been characterized by Zips (2011, p. 136) as *"clashes" of divergent habitus formations*, a *de-essentialization of identity* (p. 152), matching the *preconceived emancipatory quality of hybridization against the "conservative" or presumably reactionary tendencies of "pure authenticity"* (p. 136). Termed by Hope (2009, p. 420) as an *assimilation for survival or adaption in the face of growing pressures on the psyche of men and women who seek validity in the halls of Jamaica* and furthermore characterized *as a musical and cultural replica of the conflicted negotiations of self and identity in a materialistic world* (ibid.), the displayed slackness of Sizzla as well as the righteousness of Gangsta Ras both indicate *the historical movements in the definitions of the Rastafari self (...) within the capitalist-mediated spaces of 21st century Jamaica* (Hope, 2009, p. 412). This point of view is reflected in Marshall's (2006) remark in regard to *Hip-Hop's embrace by young Jamaicans* (p. 65) as being

> (...) consistent with a broader cultural pattern across the Caribbean, whereby American popular culture (...) has come to dominate the imaginations of young people yearning for the freedom and wealth denied to them in post- and neo-colonial circumstances and symbolized by the sensual sounds and images of Afro-Americans flaunting their power to consume (ibid.).

Referring to *the spread of Rastafari from Jamaica's lower-class to its middle-class and beyond*, Marshall (2006, p. 68) stressed its consistent and successful adaptation to historical developments and social challenges – from the death of Emperor Haile Selassie in the 1970s to the embrace of music and technology as well as the ideology's ability to change and adjust in order *to facilitate the spread of Rastafarian critiques and perspectives* (p. 68) and putting it in context with the successful re-interpretations of the Bible that the Rasta faith is build upon (p. 64). Pereira (1998) observed a trend to more spiritual lyrics on one hand and a strong socio-political emphasis on the other among Conscious Reggae artists that also had an influence on the Dancehall performers, in noting that (t)*he violence for its own sake in many of the gun lyrics now shifts increasingly towards class confrontation in the mid-nineties. Here, the consciousness of self in class and race terms merges with religious influences within a discourse of righteousness versus iniquity* (p. 35).

A turn of events, that must have been quite a surprise for those who had expected the development of a broader social theory, evolving out of the religious concept of Rastafari, *articulated and motivated by Afrocentric persons, who, though inspired by Rasta, do not necessarily share the Rasta religion* (Semaj, 2013, p. 107). This socio-political orientation, pursued through *knowledge of history, politics, economics, branding, marketing, media, and education, seasoned with the spirit of Rastafari* (p. 107) could not withstand the cleansing fire started by the triumphant arrival of the Bobo Dancehall-Rastas in the 1990s. Lamenting over the perceived decrease as a cultural force within the last thirty years, Semaj (p. 108) poses the following question:

> *Could this be the reason why the consistent greeting and refrain of the Rastaman in the first thirty years of 'peace and love' has transitioned to 'blessed', and now given way to the confrontational 'fyah bun' of the last ten years?*

Considering his hopes for an emerging Rasta-based social theory, that would *serve to make the Rastafarian religion obsolete at worst or a quaint novelty at best, now that the society has been able to successfully extract the essentially useful core of the Rastafarian faith* (Semaj, 2013, p. 96), one can very well relate to his sentiments when a considerable number of archaic preachers took the stage in storm during the 1990s. Nevertheless, the relevance and impact of Bobo Shanti doctrine spread by the *Fyah Reggae* artists on Jamaican music and the development of how Rastafarian culture is being perceived on an international level goes undisputed. As a matter of fact, *their mystical references to the cosmic fire for the wicked deeds of Babylon and its contemporary institutions* (Zips, 2006, p. 157) might even serve as a bridge for social activists, who make use of this symbolism:

> *Since these agencies are seen as identical with the 'evil forces behind globalization', the Black Bobo Ashanti movements are miraculously at one with the predominantly white anti-globalization movement that reinterprets or reinvents the 'Fire Bun' Nyahbinghi chants into revolutionary set-scenes for the dramatic struggle against the super powers ruling and allegedly destroying the world* (Zips, 2006, p. 158).

Zips furthermore considers the internationally acknowledged artists as powerful advocats of the Bobo's *claim for a right to repatriation*, which *is based on the transnational human right to repossess their homeland* (Zips, 2006, p. 157):

> *Reggae music produced by dancehall artists identifying with the Bobo Ashanti, such as Sizzla, Capleton, Anthony B., Jah Cure, or Turbulence, take these legal claims to another level, namely, the global communication network of music. Legal claims for repatriation and reparation are then supported by loud (musical) calls for 'more fire' which are easily misunderstood as support for violent action against the injustices caused by a unilateral conception of economist globalization.*

He furthermore argues that, by employing the *fyah*-vocabulary, *they actually rally for moral repentance, legal acknowledgment for the injustice commited and economic restitutions* (Zips, 2006, p. 133):

> *Seen from their perspective the word 'fire' is entirely a non-violent means to enlighten civil society consciousness in Babylon, as it currently manifests itself in the Vatican, the Pentagon, Buckingham Palace and all institutions and human actors who gained and are still gaining from the historical and continual capture of people of African origin in the Western hemisphere* (ibid.).

Expressed doctrine and ideology among Bobo Shanti artists: Similarities and differences in regard to Five Percenter Rap

A) Re-interpretation of terminology and the establishment of counterknowledge: Burning you with Words, Power and Sound

Word, sound and power is Jah way
Blessings haffi shower when we hear Jah name

Word, Sound And Power (Lutan Fyah, 2008a)

By comparing the religious doctrine and terminology of Five Percenters and Bobo Shanti, several similarities can be discovered. Both groups came up with original terms for talks, discussions or teachings as central elements for the dissemination of their traditions and doctrines, for instance – which are referred to as *reasoning* among Rasta circles and *building* in Five Percenter terminology. One might as well attest some similarity in the way that Five Percenters refer to putting facts on the table in a discussion as *dropping bombs* and the use of the Bobo's frequently invoked *fire bu(r)n!* as a means to express their rejection of information stemming from the *imperial powers* as lies. That would also imply the superior perceived religious doctrine of the Rastas based on the Old Testament as compared to the King James version of *John Paul inna di Vatican*, which is symbolically set on fire regularly by adding the aforementioned rhetorical term in Bobo ceremonies or performances of Bobo-related artists. Capleton a.k.a 'The Fireman', who originated the music that later on got labeled as *Fire Reggae* (Zips, 2011, p. 151) by frequent mentioning of the term argued that the expression – alongside the equally popular *judgment!* – is as well prominently featured in the Old Testament and standard repertoire of a typical Sunday sermon in any Jamaican church (Cooper, 2005, p. 9).

In a similar way, Bobos tend to avoid the term Africa – which is deemed a manipulative name, introduced by white colonial powers to separate them from a glorious past as Ethiopian kings or even Black Israelites, the original inhabitants of the Biblical Jerusalem (Dorman, 2016) – to define their origin. Black Muslim movements such as the Moorish Science Temple, the Nation of Islam and also the Five Percenters (Knight, 2013, p. 241) have applied a very much related empowering strategy – with the latter group insisting on being *Original Asiatic Black Man* or hailing an even more glorious past as nothing else than *Gods of the Universe* (Curtis & Sigler, 2009). While in Bible-based Rasta terminology, Africa is referred to as *Zion – the Promised Land* – and the corrupted colonial system as *Babylon* or *Rome* in return, *Father Allah's* re-defining and symbolical charging of space by turning Manhattan and Harlem into *Mecca*, Brooklyn into *Medina*, New Jersey into *New Jerusalem* or Queens into *The Desert* (Knight, 2013, p. 63) is clearly grounded on socio-historical influence of Islamic origin.

Obviously, this consistent re-interpretation of words does not stem from random occurrence but is systemetically applied out of a strong awareness for the manifold meanings and implications enclosed in words as symbols and tools for the continuation or either questioning of power structures and distributions. Rastas strongly believe in the relevance of *words, power and sounds* (Blatter, 2008, p. 19), which is frequently and prominently referred to by Reggae-artists, from recent performers like Sugar Roy & Conrad Crystal (2014) or the iconic Bobo deejay Sizzla Kalonji on his more than seventy full-length releases (Sizzla, 1997b; 2002a; 2007a).

Full time Babylon realise
Sizzla is di element of surprise
And wicked heart, I must put you down
Burning you with words, power and sound

No Other Like Jah (Sizzla, 1997b)

That idea traces back to ancient African concepts such as *Nommo*, referring to the power of the spoken word and the positive or negative forces it can bring into existence (Hamlet, 1998; Yancy, 2004; Walker & Kuykendall, 2005). Or as Leach (1966, p. 407), commenting on traditional ritualistic settings has put it: *...it is not the case that words are one thing and the rite another. The uttering of the words itself is a ritual.* With *signifyin'* (Smitherman, 1997, p. 14; Mitchell-Kernan, 1999; Khan, 2012) – *the executive technique for identity negotiation within black life* (Smith, 2007, p. 204) – a similar African trope lies at the core of the Five Percenters' trickful way of *droppin' science*, that has been described as *an expansive form of alternative language for critically tracking one's own identity against that of others within a shared milieu* (p. 204). On a structural level, the *building* in Five Percenter *ciphers* – initiated with the obligatory question 'What's today's mathematics?', that is inviting participating *Gods* to freely share their associations in regard to the respective date and the *Supreme Mathematics* – hints towards a common collective dimension and shared elements of encouraged individuality with the *reasoning* ritual as practiced in Rasta circles (Edmonds, 1998, p. 356).

Thus, the re-contextualization of words as part of a detailed semiotic analysis – described by Price (2003, p. 18) as *redefining words so that their sound aligns with its meaning* – can be attested a central meaning in both groups. Hence, Rastas would re-shape words in a way that are considered to represent their actual meaning more clear – as opposed to the attempted disguising of the *powers that be. Oppressors* would turn into *down-pressers* for instance, and *understanding* would re-manifest as *over-standing* (Slade, 2013, p. 2; Sullivan, 2007; Bell, 2011). Pollard (1982) pointed out *how the Rastafarian way of life affects the choice of term assigned to articles* (p. 36) by concluding that a *man who can label 'meat' DEADahs, is hardly a man, who eats it* (ibid.). He furthermore defined *word, sound and power* as *the command of language over consciousness, and ultimately action* (1982, p. 24) and furthermore stressed the functional use of *the forceful creative turn of words against English, the language used by the oppressor to 'increase confusion'* (p. 19). Zips (2006, p. 132) – in referring to the artistic medium of Reggae music – also emphasized *the power of the reasoning or the palaver*

> *'Words, Sounds, and Power' are therefore seen as the main means or weapon to overcome historical and contemporary forms of injustice, structural inequality, and unilateral (mis)use of (military and economic power* (Zips, 2006, p. 132).

Similarly, (b)*elieving in the subtle power of words to affect a persons's mindstate*, Father Allah a.k.a. Clarence 13X Smith *altered the language of his followers to remove all negative forces* (Knight, 2013, p. 14) in the same rigorous way, which might be illustrated by the banning of *hello* for invoking the concept of *hell* by its mentioning and the instruction to replace it with *peace*. In this line of thought, *sexism and racism could be destroyed by avoiding the words that represented them*, which resulted in the use of *'so-called men' and those who call themselves women'* – as well as *people of light complexion* for Caucasians (p. 14). Further application of these empowerment strategies can be found in the use of *Gods, earths and universes* or *sun, moon and stars* to refer to *man, woman and child*, signifying the godly descendance of the Black Man according to Five Percenter doctrine. Gibbs (2003) even suggested a direct line of this conception with the Indian cult of *Thugee*, a secretive and organized group worshipping the Indian deity Kali – the Black Goddess – who, they assumed, *sanctioned and required murder on her behalf* (p. 82), that presented a considerable threat to the colonizing claims of the British empire (ibid.):

> *It was the ontology and philosophy of the Supreme Black Goddess and its relationship to the power structure in India in the mid-1800s that brought the word 'thug' into the English language. The 'thuggish' view of power is mirrored in America today by those who live the philosophy and ontology of the 'Supreme Black God', and the 'thuggish' relationship to powers is mirrored in their respective histories.*

He furthermore stressed the important role of artists affiliated with the ideology in planting rather sophisticated, specific – and obscure, some might argue – religious concepts deep within the minds of mainstream culture consumers via highly successful musical efforts (Gibbs, 2003, p. 86-87):

> *Hit records played regularly on commercial radio hide in plain sight the religious mode of being and the metaphysics that are today's counterpart to the religious devotion of the original Thugs. This modern thug's metaphysics comes from the group commonly known as The Five Percenters.*

One of the motivations for the strong incorporation of Five Percenter terminology in Hip Hop during the late 1980s and early 1990s might simply stem from an attempt of the artists to distinguish themselves from the then popularized Gangsta Rap and add some mystery to their artistic appearance and creative output (Gosa, 2011, p. 12). On the other hand, it might as well be considered as an effective *tool of resistance and identity maintenance* for the socially underpriviliged, generating a system of codes and hidden meanings as part of a more complex alternative knowledge, questioning the interpretative sovereignty of mainstream society (p.12). As such, this carefully crafted *counterknowledge* has the power to challenge the establishment by providing *an alternative knowledge system intended to entertain while challenging white dominated knowledge industries such as academia or the mainstream press* (p. 5). Naturally, the publication of these well kept codes – that would traditionally be transferred and memorized from person to person (Gibbs, 2003, p. 91) in a teacher and initiate-context – has been met with mixed emotions by the keepers of the knowledge. When Wu-Tang's RZA – spelled out as *Ruler Zig-Zag-Zig Allah* in *Supreme Alphabet* – contributed to the de-mystification of the codes by publishing his book *The Tao of Wu* (RZA, 2009), he faced harsh criticism from within the Five Percenters for his unauthorized revealing of the movements' secret doctrine – next to supportive voices, appreciating the wide-scale dissemination of the teachings (Knight, 2013, p. 205).

Unlike certain considerations (Semaj, 2013), the terminology used by Bobo deejays – which might come across as rather aggressive for some ears – has not been introduced by these artists but gradually developed among Rastafarian circles, as demonstrated earlier. On the contrary, the coded language developed and applied by Five Percenters has been evaluated as originating a considerable amount of basic Hip Hop vocabulary (Knight, 2013, p.178), starting from the use of *G* as short for *God* – which later on has been and still is mistakenly interpreted as meaning *Gangsta*. Although Five Percenter influence could be detected around Hip Hop since its early days – the B-Boy stance later on applied by breakdancers stems from the square stance Five Percenters would form around DJs and equipment, intending to intimidate potential thieves and robbers –, it was not until the late 1980s and early 1990s that more or less clear depictions of their secret knowledge were brought to the forefront of things. However, as noted by Knight (2013, p. 186):

> *Between rap's world-wide popularity and the Five Percenters' insider language and folklore, out-right proselytism like Brand Nubian's 'Ain't No Mystery' and the esotericism of Rakim's 'The Mystery,' a God emcee can have it both ways. He can use the medium to teach the world, but while millions listen, he can also engage his Five Percenter family in a private conversation.*

B) Dogmatic perceptions and symbolism: When the Two Sevens Clash

Just as Haile Selassie is considered as the return of Jesus Christ and manifestation of God among Rastas, the Five Percenters refer to their founder Clarence 13X Smith as *Father* or simply *Allah* – which in contrast to Haile Selassie is based on his very own claim and the name he presented himself to his *first born-followers*. Both groups stress the matter of Black supremacy, and while the central teaching of the Five Percenters is the claim that *the Original Asiatic Black Man is God*, Bobo Shanti artists like Sizzla use references to royalty in titles such as *Born A King* (Sizzla, 2014) or address their Black audience as *Kings Of The Earth* (Sizzla, 1997c), as illustrated below:

Kings of the earth
Come to yuhself
Yuh cannot chase every skirt
True yuh inherit yuh wealth
Woman of the soil, where is your meditation?
Fi de black child, di future generation

Lord Jamar of Brand Nubian used the same royal claim on the track *Supreme Mathematics* (Lord Jamar, 2006a) of his programmatically titled record *The 5% Album* (2006b):

Cipher is a circle, three hundred sixty degrees
Knowledge 120, Wisdom 120, Understanding 120
A cipher is a person, place or thing
My blood line trace back to kings

This consistent pattern is as well reflected in *I.S.L.A.M.* (Lord Jamar, 2006c), with Lord Jamar's rhyme *taking my rightful place, amongst kings and queens/85's wanna know what things mean* or on *Show And Prove* (Inspectah Deck, 1999), where Wu-Tang's Inspectah Deck is encouraging Blacks to *search for knowledge, use science and math/and be kings and queens like in centuries past*. Similarly, Guru of Gangstarr makes use of the metaphor on *Above The Clouds* (Gangstarr, 1999) constructing a righteous connotation of the term by juxtaposing it with *evil factors* and *demonic chapters – I Self Lord And Master shall bring disaster to evil factors/demonic chapters, shall be captured by kings*. In what corresponds to the empowerment strategy of the Five Percenters, the Bobo Shanti as part of the Rastafarian belief claim to trace the roots of Blacks back to one of the twelve tribes of Israel, namely the tribe of Judah, as mentioned by Sizzla on *Kings Of The Earth* (Sizzla, 1997c):

The youths are royalty
No tell demself, we pick no choice
Stiff-naked fools – know yuhself, know Israelites
From the lowest of depth to the highest of height

While Bobo ideology inspires the artists to put them in a direct line with the chosen people of the Old Testament and therefore constructing their identity around Biblical parameters set by orthodox religious context, Five Percenters show a much more gnostic and radical approach in which there is little space for orthodox patterns of thought – as shown in *Wake Up* (Brand Nubian, 1990a) by Brand Nubian:

I guess I'm like the verbalizer for the fact I'm moving blackwards
This Asiatic Black Man is a dog spelled backwards
The maker, the owner, the cream of the planet Earth
Father of civilization, God of the universe

Similar to Five Percenter doctrine of the Asiatic Black Man's divine origin, Bobo affiliated artists frequently refer to the noble African descendance of their lost brothers and sisters in the Jamaican townships, as indicated by the following line of Sizzla's *Clean Up Your Heart* (Sizzla, 1998b):

Ghetto youths dey inna gang and ghetto girls dey inna a mob
We no tell de ghetto youths bout the noble heritage whey dem have

A similar perspective is presented by Sizzla on *Remember* (Taiyuan, 2008):

So come we go bun dem, ghetto kings and queens
Heathen a tremble physically rough
Mi knowledge and powers, Ethiopians dream
Inna Emperor Selassie I put all yuh trust
Yes, Black woman wake up from your dream
Inna di fantasy world, don't get stuck
Babylon, ah go turn it into a bloody scene

However, the consideration of Blacks as ancient royalty is by far not exclusive to the Bobo Shanti and can be found in various Afro-centristic movements (Curtis & Sigler, 2009; Dorman, 2016; Bascomb, 2016). Similarly, an outstanding importance given to the number Seven can be observed among both groups. For Five Percenters it is the supreme number due to the fact that within the system of the *Supreme Alphabet*, G – as the seventh letter – is coded as *God*. Wu-Tang Clan's GZA – *God Zig-Zag-Zag Allah*, known as Allah Justice in Five Percenter circles – spelled it out in *Alphabets* (GZA, 2008):

Allah Be a Born, Cee Divine, Equality
Father, then after that, there's the G-O-D

The prominence of the number is as well demonstrated by the design of the *Universal Flag*, the main visual representation of the movement, that displays a big Seven in its center, representing *the Original Man, the True and Living God, the Supreme Being, Almighty God ALLAH* (Universal Shaamgaud Allah, n.d., para. 6) or *the unification of Knowledge, Wisdom and Understanding, Man, Woman and Child* and furthermore *the male seed in full bloom* (para. 6). In the background, covered by the Seven, a crescent is visible that symbolizes Wisdom – which can refer to the wisdom manifested by Nation of Islam-founder Elijah Muhammad and further revealed by Clarence 13X Smith, or symbolize *the woman (without child)*, a *reflected light* that is *not yet at its fullest Equality* (para. 5). Next to the *Universal Flag* being prominently stretched out on the album cover of Lord Jamar's *The 5% Album* (Lord Jamar, 2006b), the symbolism is referred to frequently in lyrics of artists affiliated with the group, as in the case of Gangstarr's *Above The Clouds* (Gangstarr, 1999) – with *Seven and a half*(moon), manipulating *ten percenters* and enlightening *jewels* of true knowledge being mentioned:

The Seven and a half combined, over the front line
The ten percenters, promoting slander in the airtime
Bear in mind jewels be the tools of the trade
Sharp veins heavenly praise and dues are paid

General relevance given to the number Seven in Rasta philosophy goes back to a myth that might have been originated by Marcus Garvey (Chevannes, 1994, p. 104) about Armageddon to arrive on the 7th of July 1977, which has been popularized by Roots Reggae songs like Culture's *Two Sevens Clash* (Culture, 1977). Furthermore, Reggae artist Mr. Royal can be seen dressed up in Bobo attire in a video with Prophet Benjamin (Full Moon Films, 2015), wearing a big badge depicting a huge black Seven and a matching five-pointed star over a red, gold and green background, that is only lacking a crescent moon in order to pass for a Five Percenter emblem. On one of the Order's official websites the characteristic R for Rastafari, that is part of the Bobo Shanti flag as well, is mirrored by a Seven (www.black-king.net). In general Rasta terminolgy and symbolism, the number Seven appears in context of the *seven seals of Solomon* mentioned in Chapter Five of the Biblical *Book of Revelation*. According to Rastafarian belief, these seals have been broken by the only person deemed worthy to do so – H.I.M. Emperor Haile Selassie I, Ras Tafari, from the lineage of King David and Solomon, fulfilling prophecy as the personified *Second Coming of Christ* to reign as a rightful ruler over human affairs. Further importance is derived from Judges 16:13, in which the Biblical Nazarite Samson is characterized as having seven strands, breads or locks of hair – justifying the reverence of the number as well as providing legimitization of the dread locks grown by Rastas for spiritual purposes.

Yet another Biblical hint towards the number can be found in Hebrews 7:1, that mentions Melchizedek as King and High Priest of Salem, on which King Emmanuel I as High Priest in the Melchizedek Order had based his authority upon. Although the more moderate Rastafarian branch of the Twelve Tribes incorporated a system of reference to the number Twelve in correspondance to the number of Israelite tribes and apostles mentioned in the Bible, the equally frequently appearing Seven – as in Genesis 4:24, 5:31, 41:26, 41:27, Joshua 6:4 or the Book of Revelation 5:6 – is still granted the most special meaning among Rastas throughout different Orders. As a matter of fact, when Rastas belonging to different branches would meet, in favor for their own respective and varying customs, a greeting ritual referred to as *two sevens clash* is being used (Olivier, 2010), in which the tip of the thumb and the index finger are being joined to form two Sevens, facing each other. Haile Selassie frequently applied a similar gesture by joining his hands after his coronation, and with thumbs put slightly upwards the shape changes into a basic frame for the *Star of David* – or a signifier for the Holy Trinity in which sense it is usually applied among the Bobo Shanti adherents. The purpose is to emphasize the specific and central dogmatic conception based on Haile Selassie as God, King Emmanuel I as reincarnation of Jesus – *the Black Christ in Flesh* – and Marcus Garvey as the reincarnated John the Baptist (Barnett, 2005, p. 76), which clearly distinguishes them from other branches. Non-contextualized references to King Emmanuel I – besides from indicating the dogmatic principle of the Holy Trinity – are rather frequent among Bobo Shanti artists, such as in Lutan Fyah's *Watch Over Me* (Lutan Fyah, 2008b):

The Most High watch over me
Conquer the wicked, give I strength to carry on
Emmanuel watch over me
When dem come to destroy meh flesh, I must conquer death
(...)
The powers of the Most High
Truthfully known, the wicked man lies
I already mek my sacrifice
Hail the Black Christ, no disguise

C) Attitude towards other religious groups and ethnic discrimination: Fire Pon Rome

Drop a bomb inna di heart of Vatican and murder Babylon...

*I Will Survive (*Turbulence, 2005)

The Rasta strategy to *chant down babylon* (Davidson, 2015) as part of a wide-scale spiritual warfare against colonial powers is strongly based on the concept of *words, power and sound* and finds its expression in the infamous Nyahbinghi ceremonies, that feature *spiritual death threats to all Babylonian forces such as the Pentagon, the Vatican, Buckingham Palace and its chairholders* (Zips, 2006, p. 136), emphatically articulated over traditional drumming and chanting. Despite being clearly rooted in historical Roots Reggae topics and Nyahbinghi symbolism, the specifically aggressive delivery of the Bobo artists bears strong resemblance to the fiery – and revivalist-like (Chevannes, 1990a; Chevannes, 1994; Rommen, 2006) – sermons given by Bobo Priests during communal services in form and content. However, Bobo Priests usually would refrain from profane language, which Sizzla is actually making use of in *King In This Jungle* (Sizzla, 1997a):

Well, well, to Queen Eliza-Bitch of England
Tell yuh police no more molestation
Unnu diss King Selassie and ah pure bangarang remember
Emmanuel ah di crown champion
Mi tell yuh dis ah reach all United Nations
All now wi ah chant fi repatriation

McGlashen (2013, p. 10) has suggested that the characteristic aggression and quasi-religious militancy used by *fire burners* like Sizzla and Capleton *is equal in character to the aggression and violence evident in dancehall music,* with the habitual reference to 'the gun' (Hope, 2006) being replaced by 'fire' as a weapon of choice. Nevertheless, what sounds rather harsh and rude appears to be grounded in a deeper historical context and understanding in Rastafarian philosophy, where the praisal of Haile Selassie I as *a black monarch must be seen against the rejection of the traditional English monarchy (particulary the Queens Elizabeth I and II who are said to be whores)...* (Pollard, 1982, p. 19). In reference to the Book of Revelations as the main Biblical source for the construction of the Rastafarian ideology, Pereira (1998, p. 32) is pointing out the applied strategy of legitimization by ascribing clearly defined theological roles to the perceived contemporary sources of hope and hardships:

> *It was a relatively easy if creative and politically brilliant leap to ascribe this Kingship to Emperor Haile Selassie, and the beast and Babylon to the entire baggage of European society and culture and its historical subordination of the African. It contemporized and made real the language and meaning of ancient literature and, ironically, subverted the socio-political structures through the very book that had been used to entrench those structures.*

As a kind of more recent update from these original instrumentalizations, the names of modern day politicians – or institutions such as the United Nations, addressed by Sizzla in the above quoted excerpt – have been added on the Rastafarian list of condemnation. During the services held at the Holy Tabernacle of the Bobo Shanti settlement in Koforidua phrases like *fire burn the Queen of England* have frequently been combined with *fire burn Tony Blair – who is Tony Blair?* by the Honorable Priest Dennis Mills in order to symbolically step on the more visible and contemporary representations of imperial forces and colonial powers and question their authority. The perspective, that these signifiers are not to be confused with the actual persons is demonstrated by the fact that Tony Blair had already resigned from his position for several months at this time and the Bobos still showed no urge to replace him with his successor Gordon Brown in their litanies. Next to the defined secular targets – *the presidents and prime ministers of the former colonial powers and their relatives and successors to the world power in the United States of America* (Zips, 2006, p. 136) – of this symbolic warfare, the Nyahbinghi rituals gain their spiritual dimension from verbal attacks launched against religious representatives related to the former – most central *the Roman Catholic Pope who is pictured as the reincarnation of Satan just as Haile Selassie is God* (p. 136).

As noted by Pereira (1998, p. 35), in this context, *the consciousness of self in class and race terms merges with religious influences within a discourse of righteousness versus iniquity (...) that the image of Babylon becomes reinforced by the new icon of the Pope in John Paul II, and the associated tropes of Rome and Vatican.* Naming the involvement of the Catholic Church in the African slave trade, Rome being associated with the crucifixion of Christ, and the invasion of Ethiopia by Italy as possible reasons for historically developed (a)*nti-Papist sentiments* (p. 36), Pereira refers to the reinforcement of (l)*inguistic subversion* as *a popular Rastafarian strategy for mental emancipation* with the systematic use of inversion by citing from songs of Bounty Killer and Bobo artist Anthony B. – concluding that (t)*he singers use a strong binary model of opposition that serves to sharpen identity and resistance* (ibid.). Similar to Tony Blair, the longtime canonized John Paul II. seems to remain the personified symbolic target representing the non-secular wing of the attacked unholy union of wordly and religious enemies. In *Protect Us And Bless Us* (Sizzla, 1998c), Sizzla is accusing the Queen of England to administer injustice and inequality with the help of Christianity and the Catholic Church:

I will forever burn di wicked man, mi sure
Protect us and bless us King Emmanuel's own
Babylon killing the people, trying to control
(...)
Elizabeth of England claim the authority
To keep the people and slave the people with Christianity
And John Pope and the church dem inna conspiracy
While di Governor General ah him ah govern di money
And wi di people in di ghetto has no liberty
Give us repatriation, justice and equality

A rather shortened – but effective – simplyfication of the suggested ties between the Catholic Church and the culture of the rejected colonial powers is offered by Bobo artist Anthony B. in the form of *Fire Pon Rome* (Anthony B., 1996) – *Fire Pon Rome/Fi Pope Paul an him scissors an comb.* A similar rhetorical pattern can be found on *Genesis* (Lutan Fyah, 2011a) of his Bobo-*bredren* Lutan Fyah, who is requesting the

Pope, the Queen and their administrative helpers to acknowledge the sovereignty of Haile Selassie I and *come clean* or *get burned*:

> *Even the church haffi bow at his feet*
> *The Pope of Rome and Elizabeth, the Queen*
> *Lawyers, doctors and judges seh dem nah blaspheme*
> *Bun dem if dem nah come clean*

Considering the *quite minor denomination of Catholicism in Jamaica, attracting less than ten percent of the population* (Pereira, 1998, p. 38) – as compared to widespread Anglicism and the unarguably less prominent Archbishop of Canterbury – it has been suggested that the figure of the Pope is epitomizing, *by his European culture and race (...) the long and continuing diasporic experience of oppression* (p. 39):

> *He satisfies easily the need for differentiation, polarizing an "other" against which the African total identity can be sharpened and the historical relationship contested and overturned. There is in the image a far more concrete, contemporary, individualized and racialized association than in the older (and still current) icon of Babylon. It is a white image made familiar by the media and by the Pope's very mobility, visibility and activity* (ibid.).

The fact, that the Caribbean Council of Churches has officially accepted the Rastafarian faith into the Christian fold (Witvliet, 1985) can be seen as yet another evidence for the possibility of a symbolic reading within the context of a 'Black Christology' (Witvliet, 1987), in which the Roman Catholic Church and the papal figure are being instrumentalized as signifiers for a more complex cultural critique. A perspective, that seems to be very well supported by Sizzla's *No White God* (Sizzla, 1995):

> *I have no white God, don't teach me anything wrong*
> *Would di white God save mi from whiteman oppression*
> *I have no white God, it's just a Black Messiah*
> *If a white God a bless how him naw bless Sizz*

A logical progression of that thought can be found on his track *Bun Fire* (Sizzla, 2013a), where Sizzla is underlining the need of a *Black God* and the Biblical authority of Haile Selassie I as the rightful successor on King David's throne:

The China man praise a god weh look like him
The white man praise a god weh look like him
So we praise the Black God, the Ethiopian king
Emperor Selassie I, come seal everything
Conquering lion of the tribe of Judah, King David linage

It is worth mentioning that according to the Honorable Priest Henry, Empress Menen – the wife of Haile Selassie I, was a descendant of the Prophet Muhammad (s.a.s) and their marriage therefore symbolized the reunion of the House of Isaac and the House of Ismael. On the other hand, the rather aggressive rejection of Jesus Christ by Bobo artists has led to attacks from other Rastafarian groups who pointed out that – since Haile Selassie I is considered a reincarnation of Christ – it would implicate a rejection of His Imperial Majesty as well, in consequence (rasorder, 2009). Confronted with accusations that being anti-Christ is being anti-Selassie in the cited video, Capleton stated that nobody can burn the Emperor and he doesn't burn Christ, he is burning Jesus and acknowledges the Black Christ instead – which may be read as a form of cultural critique in the shape of reversed racism, similar to Sizzla's lines in *Show Us The Danger* (2013b):

We are di foundation of dis earth
Black people, we wrote di Bible first
Christ is from our lineage
Black man is the Christ, read the Bible, you'll find it

However, a direct variation of the theme that is based on a common pattern of Black Muslim exegesis (O'Connor, 1998) presents itself on Lord Jamar's *Deep Space* (Lord Jamar, 2006d) – on which Wu-Tang's RZA is equaling the revering of a white Messiah with ignorance in the course of his guest appearance. Although in full accordance to the teachings of Five Percenters as well as with the concept of Haile Selassie I as the reincarnation of Christ in Rastafarian belief and King Emmanuel I as the *Black Christ in Flesh* among the Bobo Shanti, the line *Helped find God in man, like Emmanuel* refers to the Biblical mentioning of the Hebrew name in this case:

I was a mommy's boy, soft, Uncle Tommy Boy
Walking the streets, like a dead zombie, boy
Swine eating, lying, cheatin, praying to a white Jesus
Never thought the first man on earth, it could be us
Got blessed with the twelve jew-els, learned they could do me well
Helped find God in man, like Emmanuel
Who's the original, who's the grafted criminal
Who crafted trick knowledge, to attack the subliminal
Subconscious stages, I got the book, turned the pages
Learned one hundred and twenty, and nine phases
Of the moon, stay in tune, all praises due
The truth is what raises you

The depiction of a historical figure that is supposed to be of Hebrew origin as a fair-haired, blue-eyed persona does bear traces of colonial instrumentalization, however, and can be seen as but one element of a more complex campaign to establish and justify concepts of superiority and inferiority, as suggested in Gangstarr's *Conspiracy* (Gangstarr, 1992):

You've got to understand that this has all been conspired
To put a strain on our brains so that the strong grow tired
It even exists when you go to your church
'cause up on the wall a white Jesus lurks

The rather sophisticated understatement of *Conspiracy* is contrasted by a more militant and radical stance that Brand Nubian is taking on *Ain't No Mystery* (Brand Nubian, 1993a), where rapper Lord Jamar raised claims of Black divinity and accused the Catholic Church to be involved in hiding that matter – therefore threatening to *buy a tec* – a semi-automatic pistol – and open fire in the Vatican, in close resemblance to patterns of spiritual warfare practiced by the Bobo Shanti:

Who's the clown, that didn't paint Jesus brown?
Everybody knows the man was original
When the jam is over I'ma go and take my vegetable
Check buy a tec let loose in the Vatican
Courts writin' lies, record company is mad again
These Asiatic is racist
Because I love the Black faces
So put your Bible in the attic cause I didn't come for static
The True and Living G-O-D
It ain't no mystery

In regard to discrimination concerning ethnical origin, the two groups differ in various aspects. Although both of them are based on the principle of Black supremacy, this position must be considered more as a theoretical assumption than actual practice. Despite whites being labeled as devils frequently among Black Muslim movements, as opposed to the Nation of Islam, the Five Percenters have seen white initiates such as the infamous Azrael, who has been given the knowledge by *Father Allah* Clarence 13X Smith himself during their common stay at a mental hospital in the 1960s, or the frequently referred to Michael Muhammad Knight (a.k.a. Azrael Wisdom). According to dominant Five Percenter doctrine, white members are not able to be granted the God-attribute but are considered righteous, as opposed to the ignorant eighty-five percent of the population (Knight, 2013, p. 231). The same way that Five Percenters are eager to make clear that they are *neither muslims nor anti-white or pro-black* (p. 6), the Bobo Shanti show no exclusive tendencies towards whites whatsoever. As opposed to Five Percenter circles, whites may as well undergo the training process and achieve the equal status as Priests that Blacks are given in the Order. As a matter of fact, during conversations with the Honorable Priest Ferdinand at the Bobo compound in Koforidua/Ghana, a recent visit of a European convert to the faith, known as Bobo Markus, who is active as a missionary and Priest in Europe has been mentioned. The Honorable Priest Ferdinand furthermore stated that although revering the black color as good and the white color as evil, Bobos do not apply this principle to the color of the skin but the color of the heart. Therefore, to him, a white man with a Black heart would be preferable over a white-hearted Black man.

Seen from that point of view, Barnett's (2006) observation concerning the claim *that the Rastafari movement has now been deracialized could only really be leveled at the Twelve Tribes of Israel house and at the widely contested Coptic house* (p. 876) seems to be in need of reconsideration. Similarly, references of the white man being Satan during speeches of King Emmanuel I (Chevannes, 1994, p. 70) can only be seen from a symbolic, theoretical perspective with the purpose to establish and justify the liberating conception of Black supremacy. As a matter of fact, Chevannes (1990b) has demonstrated the role of Rastafarian thought in the overcoming of racist ideology in Jamaica. Bobo artists such as Lutan Fyah in their turn frequently stress their respect for all races in their output, as in the introduction to *More Blessings* (Lutan Fyah, 2015a):

> (...) *we have some blessing for each and everyone of you. whether you're black, whether you're white, whatever religion, whatever political views. you know we're all one - one people, one family, together we stand. one for all, all for one, operate in that manner. no failure.*

However, in terms of tolerance towards competing branches of the respective group there are significant differences to observe. The relations between the Five Percent Nation and the Nation of Islam as well as Sunni Islam, the Moorish Science Temple and all of the numerous offsprings have been characterized by harsh confrontational politics and violent clashes – as well as strategic cooperational patterns (Knight, 2013, p. 96). Nevertheless, Hip Hop artists related to the Five Percenters frequently use utterances of respect for the Nation of Islam in their artistic output and within the Hip Hop community the feude seems to be less present than in prison yards, for instance (p. 167). A Five Percenter mistakenly taken for a Sunni due to his Muslim headgear would respond to the phrase *as salam alaikum* not with the expected *wa alaikum salam* but with a heretic *peace, God* (p. 14.) – thus clearly distancing himself from *al-Islam* and paving the way for possible confrontational assaults. In so far, it is rather surprising that Brand Nubian's Grand Puba – in a quite integrationist manner – explicitly insists on using the traditional greeting formula among orthodox Muslims for the salutation of *brothers* on *Drop The Bomb* (Brand Nubian, 1990b):

The devil is the one who dare not to unite us
Brought forth the plan on how to divide us
Jamaicans, Christians eatin' bacon, when I greet my brothers
I say, 'Assalaam alaikum!'

On the other hand, Brand Nubian repeatedly displayed a somewhat confusing attitude in that regard by their frequent references to *al-Islam*. The band sampled a recording of a Muezzin calling the *Adhan* – the call for the ritual prayer – on a song entitled *Allah U Akbar* (Brand Nubian, 1993b), which Knight (2013, p. 179) attested, *may be misconstrued as binding them to al-Islam* – not without shifting attention to the *translingual breaking-down,* in which *the Arabic* Allahu Akbar *(God is the Greatest) finds a new meaning as 'Allah U Akbar'* (p. 179), basically addressing the *Gods* in the second form, singular – that qualifies to arouse criticism for idol worshipping from orthodox Muslims (Swedenburg, 1996, p. 2). The artists furthermore apply the salutation of *as salam alaikum* in a regular manner on their recording *One for All* (Brand Nubian, 1990c) – which has been demonstrated to be usually avoided by Five Percenters, who do not consider themselves to be a religious movement and do not see Sunni Muslims as part of the righteous five percent of the population (Knight, 2013). Lord Jamar only adds to the confusion by referring to his creative output as *Jihad music* and implying his adherence to *Islamic law* in the following lines of *I.S.L.A.M.* (Lord Jamar, 2006c):

Black Man, the colored man is the European
Ran up to his cave, he was fleeing
Over hot sand, steal from me and I chop hands off
That's Islamic law

However, Wu-Tang Clan's Raekwon delivers similarly contradicting and confusing verses on Lord Jamar's *Original Man* (Lord Jamar, 2006e), jumping from ritual Muslim prayer *at the mosque* to the utilization of *stacks* of money for balancing structural racism and celebrating of capitalist culture alike, back to *ugly, bugsy, rugby thugs* to end with *Allah is One* – the central testimony of orthodox Muslims:

We at the mosque prayin', nickel bags of black
Foto stacks, it's ganja season
(...)
We gon'show the government it ain't about Blacks
It's only 'bout stacks
Furnish labs, ballin' crabs, Houston Oiler mask
Reebok, tennis yellow, fellow goin' mad
(...)
Back to the filthy, ugly, bugsy rugby thugs
With no love, slugs, silver ones throw these
Split niggas temples, forget, the shit's freshly squeezed
Roll that Nestle, the vet's seen in rentals
Fly language, lick the sawed-off and spray you
Aiyo, Allah is One, I'm done, no playin', nigga

As a matter of fact, the main point of conflict between Five Percenters and other Muslim groups would be the reference to their founder as *Allah* and the consideration of themselves as *Gods*. On the contrary, despite their reclusive tendencies and rather rigid interpretations of the Rastafari philosophy, Bobo Shanti adherents tend to be more or less accepted among the other main branches of the faith and usually keep respectful relations with them on their behalf. This is quite interesting though, since the religious doctrine of the Bobos is going beyond orthodox interpretations by granting the divine attribute not only to Haile Selassie but to Bobo founder King Emmanuel I as well. That could be perceived as blasphemous by adherents of Rasta othodoxy and may have easily led to tension between the groups. Despite these conceptional differences, Bobo artists like Capleton, Sizzla, Anthony B., Lutan Fyah or Jah Mason usually do not raise claims of exclusivity for their interpretation, nor do they condemn other Rastafari Mansions, such as the Twelve Tribes or Nyahbinghi.

As demonstrated by Olivier (2010), who defined the Bobo Shanti as *a rapidly growing and exclusive group, who practise strict Old Testament Mosaic Rituals and Laws* (p. 128), mutual respect between Rastafarian sects resulted in specific greeting rituals, that are applied whenever members of different groups would meet. As mentioned earlier, Rastas would touch each others index finger and thumb, to form a gesture that has been used by Haile Selassie, referred to as *Two Sevens Clash*. However, next to ongoing tensions among the different Houses of Rastafari evolving around *idiosyncratic differences and personal feuds* (Semaj, 2013, p. 105), Bobo artists occasionally distance themselves rather clear from Rastas who neglect cultural aspects and tend to live the philosophy more like a lifestyle than a religion – sometimes to please females in the context of sex tourism (Spiteri, 2014) – as criticized by Lutan Fyah in *Trials And Crosses* (Lutan Fyah, 2011b):

Hey, mi nah be no giggalo
Mi nah go g-spot it
Mi no seaside dread
Mi no rental fi tourist
Hypocrites dem betta know dis!

A pattern, that can be found in Capleton's *Bun Dung Dreddie* (Capleton, 2000) as well, who is linking the deviant sexual services – the term *bow* refers to shunned sexual practices – offered by the *rent-a-dread* to drug abuse, condemning it as a form of collaboration with the colonial powers in what is part of a more complex cultural criticism:

Nuff rent-a-dread ah bow pon the North coast
Bow to the Queen
Bow to the Pope
Under the influence of the thing called the dope

Efforts of distinguishing themselves from those who consider their Rastafarian appearance a simple fashion statement are rather frequent on recordings of Bobo artists. On *Bun Fire* (Sizzla, 2013a), Sizzla is addressing those wearing Rasta locks as a fashion style and showing up in *clubs* and *pubs* without participating in the religious and spiritual rituals of the culture – such as the infamous Nyahbinghi ceremonies in the *Holy Tabernacle*, for instance:

Bun fire pon men weh have locks and still nah go Rastaman Tabernacle, yeah
If you don't chant Nyahbinghi then we can't win the battle
(...)
You see dem in the clubs and you see dem in the pubs
And they never ever step beneath the Tabernacle roof

Since their collective identity – unlike the more heterogenous Five Percenters – is rather well defined, Bobo artists give a lot of space to claims of authenticity. Although demonstrating an inclusive attitude towards other branches of the faith, in *Bun Dung Dreddie* (Capleton, 2000), Capleton still points out central Bobo characteristics such as the homogenous, non-Western and religiously inspired dress code and overall non-fashion appearance as a distinctive element of authenticity and excellence – separating the *wolf from the sheep flock* and the *lion* from the *fox*:

Call Nyabinghi, Twelve Tribes, Orthodox
Pass mi the tick and put the fire pon de ah
Call Bobo Ashanti from the hill top
Seperate the wolf dem from the sheep flock
Man ah real Congo Natty, man ah nuh curly locks
(...)
Nuff of dem ah lion but mi see seh dem fox

On the other hand, with distinction from those not really taking part in the culture being achieved, the Rastafarian territory itself remains a quite competitive area at times, with more liberal, open branches being looked down at by the rather strict Bobos, that are being considered the most reclusive, communal and churchical in nature (Barnett, 2002, p. 58). A fact, that does not go unnoticed by more moderate, socially oriented artists, such as Beenie Man, who acknowledged the achievements of the Order under the guidance of King Emmanuel I but criticized separatist developments after the latter past away on *Selassie* (Beenie Man, 2001):

Inna 1957 when tings just a settle down
When a near independence and Selassie never come
Outta back a wall a whey di Bobo camp did settle down
Housing sheme did all a build up
Tings a bulldozer dung
Emmanuel mek a wall and a Bull Bay di man tun
Whey him build a di Bobo camp and everyone was welcome
Outta Marcus Garvey a tun him eyes pon Kingston
Whey him build di Bobo camp and everyone was welcome
Bobo camp an institution for di old and young
For historical fact, go deh go siddom
43 years of work everything overcome
Now Emmanuel dead, everything tumble down
The Hill divided in a three, separated bu three sons
Middlesex, Priest Donavan rule the daughters and the sons
Over Surrey, Priest Lennon a pure fire him man
Priest Mallard gone a prison fi nearly bun di hill dung
Right now a one million Bobo deh a Jamdown
Selassie seh before one a him word shall pass
Heaven and earth shall bun up like a ball
Tell mi whey di hell a gwaan a Dancehall
Build more brisge and bruck dung all wall

Beenie Man – who is speaking out against the divison of the faith into different branches on *Protect Me* (Beenie Man, 1999) as well – has been criticized by Capleton for watering down the core concept of Rastafari as a strategy for Black resistance against Western imperialism by trying to merge it with mainstream Christianity in order to reach or maintain a broader audience after his conversion to the faith:

Rasta a move like men and people, eno
All dem get up and do a fight dem one another
Bobo a fight 'gainst Shanti and di Bingie I dem
A fight 'gainst di Twelve Tribe, but hear mi nuh
(...)
We, a di whole a we deh inna Selassie family, but Jah

The rather edgy, aggressive approach of the Bobo Shanti artists does not go uncontested among the more moderate Rastas, who pursue a more cultural and philosophical understanding of the faith which is conflicting with the outspoken religious identity and rigid behavior of the Bobo Shanti Order, which leads artists like Midnite to link them with radical extremist Taliban in *Enough For Everyone* (Midnite, 2001):

You know wreck age man, you know scientific intervention
If them coulda just see something and lef um
You know narcissism side effects inna them central vision
You know some man favor Bobo Shanti Taliban
And we still 'ave enough for everyone

The portrayal of Bobos as *the Jamaican Taliban* among artists and journalists has led to a number of reactions in the creative output of its members in the music business, who often take a vigorous stand against these claims – as in the case of Lutan Fyah's *Length Of Days* (Jamaica Explosion Hd, 2010):

Dey seh we're cursed
Come show them, seh we blessed
Mi no Bobo Shanti Taliban
Don't call me no ruff-neck

Although the tightly wrapped and colorful turban of the Bobo Shanti clearly differs from the ones the Taliban are using, Bobo artist Junior Reid named the typical headgear as a clear trigger for this case of mistaken identity. Next to his declaration of *you see mi turban, don't make it cause no disturbance* in *Hat Over Turban* (Junior Reid, 2002a), he dedicated a whole tune with the title *Man A Nuh Taliban* (Junior Reid, 2002b), to the issue:

Just di other day mi make a trip, go a foreign land
Reach di airport I went mi talk to immigration
Dem sight di Ras, dem sight mi turban
Dem seh Taliban, dem seh Taliban
(...)
Dey seh where you was at the time of da bombing
Mi and my girlfriend, locked up in a cabin
If dem a wonder if I'm Muslim guy
Tell dem dis a guy dis a nuh Arab guy

D) Visibility and declared affiliation of artists

Due to the fact that compared to more moderate Rasta Mansions (Chakravarty, 2014a) the Bobo Shanti Order is a quite homogenous group that considers aspects of physical appearance as well as appropriate behavior as rather relevant, most Bobo artists clearly distinguish themselves from other musicians. Although artists like Lutan Fyah, Capleton or Jah Mason tend to be quite consistent in following the dress code suggested by the Order, others like Sizzla – whose attitude towards fashion seems to be as versatile as his approach to making music – are frequently dressed up in suite and tie or casual loose sports gear. His wearing of gold and silver bracelets or necklaces is in clear opposition to the strict Bobo teachings that regard these objects as symbols of shackles and chains used during slavery times. While Rasta artists affiliated with the Twelve Tribes would typically – but not necessarily – choose dreadlocks as a hairstyle, for adherents of the Nyahbinghi branch it is compulsory to grow dreads (Barnett, 2005) and Bobos are expected to on top of it strictly follow the convention of *covering the crown* (Chevannes, 1994, p. 176; Kamimoto, 2015, p. 35) – in order to conceal their dreadlocks *from the unbelievers*, as the Honorable Priest Henry has put it. Similarly, in their early days, Five Percenters often embraced an Afrocentric identity, encouraged by their founding father, who *embraced Afrocentrism and sometimes wore dashikis; his Suns, often with African names such as Yamuse and Uhoso, adopted a trademark Five Percenter 'crown', a knit kufi with one tassel* (Knight, 2013, p.112).

However, before being granted entrance to the Bobo compound in Koforidua, any kind of headgear has to be taken off, since the privilege to cover the hair is exclusive to trained Priests. The importance given to hairstyle, attire and headgear is reflected in the corresponding use of *Congo Natty*, *robe* and the turban as the *royal hat* in Capleton's *Bun Dung Dreddie* (Capleton, 2000):

Man ah real Congo Natty
Man ah no curly locks
Can't dis the Bobo and seh the Bobo wear frock
Can't see the king if you no royal hat
Royalness haffi the royal flock
Robe and turban fi de royal flock
No Mosscini, Versace and dress like ah ass
Nuff of them ah lion but me see seh dem ah fox

Similar hints of supremacy associated with the characteristic Bobo headgear can be found on Sizzla's *King In This Jungle* (Sizzla, 1997a), where the superiority of the Bobo turban over more conventional caps and tams worn by members of other branches is being stressed:

From yuh sight di Bobo man tek off your tams and do it
Yuh sight the turban tek off you caps dem and do it
Sight Emmanuel, every empress must be neat
Yuh sight King Selassie, Babylon gon beneath

Junior Reid has dedicated a whole song – *Hat Over Turban* (Junior Reid, 2002a) – to the matter of the Bobo turban, strongly underlining the central importance of the headgear among the community:

When you put on your turban
You surpass the world of wearing hat or cap
(...)
Since Emmanuel moved, every man want to cover up a cap
Hat over turban, got I sigh and wonder
Dem should a ask questions, dey would have get di answer
(...)
Enough men dem neva mek a broom
And dem are on Jerusalem school room
Enough men nuh wanna mek no marks
Seh, don't run away from the royal dutt, remember dat

The Bobo Shanti turban is seen as a significant distinguishing symbol that is considered as superior to wordly powers, as lined out by Sizzla in *One Away* (Sizzla, 1997d):

Yuh see the Prime Minister know what a galong
A dem sell out di yutes to the Queen a England
Di whole a dem haffi bow when dem see mi turban
(...)
Dem sight mi turban, conspiracers a talk
Emmanuel, so watch out because him a guh wrath

In this context it is noteworthy that other subdivisions of the Rastafarian faith in general give less importance to hairstyle and headgear, but would cover their hair for ceremonial purposes. However, the Honorable Priest Henry explained that the importance given to the turban as a symbol for a royal crown goes back to the shared Israelite traditions of Jesus Christ and other prophets supported by the power of *truth and rights* on their *rightful journey*. The adaptation of the Biblical vow of the Nazarite to not cut one's hair during a period of life solely occupied with divine service is but another example of Christian influence (Chakravarty, 2014b). Many Rastas see themselves as the original Christians in the tradition of Jesus Christ, stick to the Old Testament and reject the Roman Catholic church. Therefore, the Honorable Priest Henry referred to the Bobo turban as an important insignia, pointing to the self-conception of being righteous and just inheritors of prophetic traditions.

Interestingly, this conception corresponds with the high reverence the turban is given in Muslim tradition as *the crown of Islam* (Kister, 2000; Jauhiainen, 2008; Goldish, 2009; Şarlak, Onurel, Koleksiyon, & Kayıt, 2014). Sufi Orders such as the Mevlevi or Naqshbandi consider their characteristic hats to be tombstones – as a symbol for them being dead for this world and ready to enter the afterlife anytime. Additionally, they intend to permanently carry their shroud with them in form of a neatly wrapped turban that is supposed to be seven meters in length in order to fulfill its purpose properly (Kabbani, 2003; Stjernholm, 2011). In correspondence to that, the Honorable Priest Henry further explained that the tightly wrapped turban – whose adjustment is seen as a kind of meditation itself – signifies the intention of the Priest to remain tight and firm in regard to wordly matters and material temptations. Therefore, wearing the turban represents a privilege among the Bobo Shanti that is linked to certain requirements, due to the specific meaning attached to it – in which it differs from the above mentioned Islamic traditions, however (Kamimoto, 2015, p. 45):

> (...) *after studying the doctrine for roughly three months, they are allowed to wrap their dreadlocks in turbans and to wear robes. EABIC members insist that a man donning a turban represents God in the flesh; therefore, upon earning the privilege of wearing a turban, a member must not remove it in public.*

Overall proper appearance is a must for Bobos who associate themselves with cleanliness – since *cleanliness is next to Godliness*, as the Honorable Priest Ferdinand stated in accordance to the teachings of the Order. Therefore, the shirt has to be neatly tucked into the pants in order to attain a humble and decent presentation. Loose, sagging pants – as popularized by Hip Hop artists – are considered to be associated with an improper lifestyle. As noted by Gibbs (2003) in reference to prison inmates not being allowed to wear belts for security reasons, *deconstructive fashionistas remark on the paradox that hip-hop's stereotypical fashion statement comes from jail – men without freedom providing the dress code for men with all the freedom and luxury capital in the world* (p. 82). Due to the practice of recruiting members among criminals and prisoners, tattoos are quite widespread among Five Percenters but severely shunned as *Bismarcks* by Bobos in reference to European colonial powers invading the African continent – bringing along their *pagan Roman ways and practices*, according to the Honorable Priest Ferdinand.

Although Bobo artists are supposed to permanently wear the characteristic turban, most of them do not strictly follow the overall dress code and make use of all kind of fashionable elements. In this context, Hope (2009, p. 408) suggests a *cross-fertilization with fashioned, coiffed hip hop artistes* as a possible reason for these developments.

Bobo women are expected to cover their arms and legs (Chevannes, 1994, p. 176), in reverence to Empress Menen Asfaw, the wife of Haile Selassie I. During periods of ceremonial worship the Bobo Priests would put on long, flashy robes in red, gold, and green or plain white.

Five Percenters on the contrary seem to give little to no relevance to clothing and may not be as easily identified by outer appearance, but according to Knight (2013, p. 218) often wear informal, fashionable street gear. He furthermore suggested that although Malcolm X's rebellious attitute and revolutionary talk always has been naturally appealing to Black youths, most of them would refrain from joining the Nation of Islam due to their strict and formal dress code (Barnett, 2002, p. 55) and strongly reject giving up street wear in exchange for a bowtie (Knight, 2013, p. 64). Among Five Percenters anything goes – at least on the man's side. Women are expected to cover their bodies and usually wear colorful and flashy cloth wrapped around their heads. In sharp contrast to the Nation of Islam and the teachings of Elijah Muhammad, who in 1968 had banned female attenders dressed in traditional African attire – sharply condemning it as a degrading adoption of uncivilized jungle dwellers (Knight, 2013, p. 112) – (t)*he brightly colored headwraps worn by many Five Percenter 'Queens' owe less to Islamic dictates of* hijab *than to the late-1960s boom of interest in African history and culture* (p. 112).

A casual shout-out to King Emmanuel I is common practice among Bobo artists and considerable portions of structured lyrical content are dedicated to the Order, providing vast space for the dissemination of moral judgments, ideological concepts and praisal of lifestyle. Five Percenters among Hip Hop artists on the other hand tend to remain less visible, to a certain degree due to the heterogenous character of the group, that knows little recognizable or identifiable patterns of behavior and appearance. Declared affiliation with the ideology is rather rare, however, it is more likely that the *Gods* (and *Earths*) among the rappers just drop discrete hints in coded language, directing their speech to an in-crowd of initiated listeners (McMurray, 2007).

But then again, Brand Nubian recorded a version of the *Universal Anthem* – the official Five Percenter hymn, intonated at every gathering – as *Allah & Justice* (Brand Nubian, 1993c), made extensive use of Five Percenter symbolism in video clips like *Wake Up* (Atlantic Records, 2009) and even chose the movement's headquarter – the *Allah school in Harlem* – as a location for the video shoot. The same goes for their appearance on the popular show *Yo! MTV Raps* (deejayedyk, 2012), that focused heavily on the Five Percenter background of the artists, including footage from inside the school and a lecture-style speech, breaking down the teachings to a mass audience. The same is true for the video to *Allah U Akbar* (Threatrics The 3rd, 2013), that depicted Five Percenter-elder Born Justice Allah teaching a class in the lecture room of the *street academy* (Knight, 2013, p. 179). Due to more strict regulations concerning the use of recording equipment in remotive Bobo Shanti settlements, affiliated artists are basically limited to make use of shots from outside the compound, leaving spectators guessing what is actually happening behind the flashy fence painted in red, gold and green colors. Nevertheless, Bobo artists are providing considerable space in their work to drop references to the Order, with Sizzla having entitled one of his albums *Bobo Ashanti* (Sizzla, 2000a) or Junior Reid's prominently placed membership declaration in the title of his recording *Emmanuel Calling* (Junior Reid, 2000).

Although Bobos in Koforidua are met with respect and seem to not face any rejection among the residents of the nearby village, locals would usually stay away from the compound, partly due to the severe and strict enforcements of expected conduct. However, as pointed out by Zips (2006, p. 156), *the popularity of Rasta reggae in Ghana, considered by most as a genuine local music instead of a Jamaican or Caribbean musical tradition, facilitates a cultural communication over language barriers and different historical experiences*. Despite of that, involvement of Bobos in the music industry is still regarded as cooperating with the capitalistic, *imperialist Babylonian system* of oppression by many followers. Kamimoto (2015, p. 44) argued that *Rastafari was introduced to the world by reggae music, which is a 'global commodity'*.

> *As such, we can see traces of colonialism in reggae music as it is distributed by global record companies, most of which are based in North America and Europe. (...) Given that Rastafari has been verbalising, visualising and criticising the colonial power relationship (...) it is very natural that tensions would emerge between reggae and Rastafarians* (ibid.).

Nevertheless, there is certain evidence that King Emmanuel I considered the wide-scale popularity of the music as a valuable strategic item for the dissemination of his cause, as suggested by Zips (2006, p. 130):

> *Some of the best known proponents, such as Capleton and Sizzla were instructed in the Bobo Ashanti teachings by leading priests of the 'Congress' (short for Ethiopia Africa Black International Congress Church of Salvation) in order to utilize the power and global range of reggae for an effective campaign towards the materialization of repatriation.*

This notion, however, has been reported in a somewhat contrasting manner by Kamimoto (2015, p. 47), who stated that (t)*hose of the older generation often say that the influence of Bobo deejays has grown, and has not had a positive effect*:

> *Several elders told me King Emanuel thought that Nyahbinghi was the only Rastafarian music; he had a negative opinion of reggae music. On the other hand, he did not prohibit reggae musicians such as Capleton and his heralds such as Junior Reid from converting* (ibid.).

Kamimoto concluded to attest *that the status of Bobo deejays is marginal within the EABIC* (2015, p. 47), pointing out that negative perceptions *sometimes derive from not only the character of reggae, but also the behaviour of Bobo deejays* (p. 47) – referring to a dynamic stage acting that is rather conflicting with the settled code of conduct within the community, where members *are not allowed to display intemperate behaviour* (ibid.). Another point of criticism Bobo artists have to face from the community is that their profession makes it quite impossible for them to keep the central custom of honoring the Sabbath by attending services and abstaining from worldly matters (Kamimoto, 2015, p. 48), which is why they are often considered as spiritually inferior members. Others complained that some of them just leave the community as soon as they had enough training to get the permission to wear a turban and never come back – or criticized that even *more deejays were wearing turbans without the EABIC's permission and self-proclaiming their EABIC-membership* (p. 48).

Although valuing *the success of the Bobo deejays, in that they were spreading the name of Bobo Shanti and knowledge about it*, as well as acknowledging *that Bobo deejays are fascinating people*, many members expressed their opinion towards Kamimoto *that they were immature in terms of spirituality* (2015, p. 48). This matter is illustrated by the fact that although numerous members switched from the traditional broom production to the manufacturing of hand-crafted pins and amulettes – so-called *guidances*, with more and more of them bearing the faces of Sizzla or Capleton instead of the traditional Rasta motives –, they strongly refrain from wearing them on themselves. From their point of view, *because they were superior to Bobo deejays in terms of spirituality, they did not require the protection of Bobo deejays* (p. 49). Despite of this, Bobo artists frequently present themselves as self-styled protectors of *the Bobo youth* in their songs, as is the case with Sizzla's *Like Mountains* (Sizzla, 2002b):

Ey, journalist, just get this inna your clippers
Nah dis the Bobo youth whey ah fling heavy powers

Intentionally or not, Sizzla's claim – *the Bobo youth, I love them from a distance* – on *Lovely Morning* (Sizzla, 1998d) pretty much signifies the push-and-pull type relationship between the beloved youngsters and their somehow less appreciated father figures. The young Priests in training at the Bobo settlement in Koforidua held similar views towards Reggae music in general and the hybrid Dancehall-Reggae of the mentioned Bobo artists specifically. The only music they would allow themselves to listen to was Nyahbinghi, which they deemed as sacred. Others, like the Honorable

Priest Ferdinand, expressed their appreciation for Roots Reggae artists like Bob Marley but did not deem it worthy to engage in listening to such music. Sizzla explicitly expressed himself in defense of Reggae music on his track *Oneness* (Akam Entertainment, 2013), however:

Music brings the Oneness
An no matter how Babylon a fight
Ghetto youths just be honest
Remember to love and unite
(...)
Well, ghetto girls deh ou dem hot an
Ghetto youths tell you seh him a the top man
Righteousness cyaan stop man
Wi taking it straight to the top an
That is why reggae music rock an
Long time mi si seh dem fight against black man
Reggae music lock down the block an
Wi left dem inna shock
(...)
Reggae music a the youths dem living
Badmind people ain't got nothing giving
(...)
Music meck the youths dem come together
A the truth yo hear mi now, you a mi brother
Meck music, meck lyrics, and go and get treasue
Number one song bring the treader

According to Zips, in the wake of *the tremendous success of Bobo Ashanti, or so-called 'Fire'-reggae, the leadership of the Congress decided to enter the music production scene on its own* (2006, p. 133) by releasing albums with *hymns of worship and chants of redemption accompanied by 'churchical' Nyahbinghi drumming* (p. 130), in order to gain in a less secular way from the financial benefits that the ambivalently viewed artists had brought upon them. He furthermore evaluates this step as signifying *a dynamic change in political strategies since the Bobo Ashanti house had so far shunned commercial recordings of their spiritual music* (ibid.). However, it is worth mentioning that the Bobo Shanti produced several videos in which they officially condemn Reggae music (empresss1n3, 2011; Boboorder, 2012).

When it comes to how to deal with the financial aspects of life, the positions of Five Percenters and Bobo Shanti present themselves to be slightly different – with Wu-Tang rapping iconic lines such as *Cash Rules Everything Around Me – C.R.E.A.M., get da money, singing dollar bill* (Wu-Tang Clan, 1993) and Lutan Fyah's declaration *Watch it, let mi clear mi conscious, give Emmanuel, the children, one thenth* (*Ghetto Stress*, Lutan Fyah, 2004). Money is not considered as negative among Five Percenters and children are educated and brought up to participate in well-paid and socially respected professions – with the Harlem based *Allah School in Mecca* bearing the classification as *street academy* in its subtitle, thus underlining the orientation towards social mobility (Knight, 2013, p. 187). Few of the children who attended the *Jerusalem School Room* on *Zion Hill*, the Bobo Shanti headquarter in Bull Bay, Jamaica, continue their education in a state-run institution – mostly due to the a rather limited choice in permitted, mostly farming- and handicraft-based occupations, as defined by King Emmanuel I (Kamimoto, 2015). Social status is not seen as conflicting with Five Percenter identity on the other hand and although the ideology emerged, spread and still heavily recruits in a social environment where criminal activities are common, like Sadat X put it, the point is to be *known by college grads* (Brand Nubian, 1998a) and positively change one's self-perception from jail convicts to *intelligent brothers* in *college dorms* – as Lord Jamar put it in *Original Man* (Lord Jamar, 2006d):

The Nation of the Five Percent, rap sent
Intelligent brothers, to represent
Allah Justice made the knowledge born
You find the Gods from the jails to the college dorms

College dorms, that produced more intellectual Five Percent rapper like J-Live – also known as Justice Allah – who, although far from the raw street appeal of the Wu-Tang Clan, still puts his ideological influence on full display in lyrics such as *The Best Part* (J-Live, 1998):

True school styles light up the night like Times Square
GZA said it, this ain't an eighty-five affair
It's the grand opening of a long career
(...)
Supreme mathematics is now the translator
As the stakes and the skills and the love became greater
For an artform to spread from East to Westside
The coast, the hemisphere, look how Hip Hop grew
But it's still the proverbial sad clown of music
Exploited by many, understood by few

While Hip Hop superstars such as Raekwon and Ol' Dirty Bastard provided financial means to run and develop the schooling activities of *Allah's street academy* and big name rappers are as welcome as anyone else on the premises, it is quite safe to say that the contrast between international stardom of Bobo artists and the simple lifestyle of their ordinary *bredren* – trying to make a living by selling handmade broomsticks that are supposed to represent physical and spiritual cleanliness – could hardly be bigger. At this point it is worth to note, that the often ridiculed broom manufacturing refers back to the self-conception of Bobos as Israelites, who were restricted to *procuring straw to manufacture bricks* during Egyptian captivity (Chevannes, 1994, p. 187). While it is quite difficult to determine to which degree the fame and success of the artists is related to their extensive use of Bobo symbolism and rhetoric or their mere musical talents in respective, the fact that they are making money with something that is basically rejected by the Bobo elders as part of the exploitative and manipulative structures established by the colonial-imperial oppressors of the *Babylonian system* can only be seen as a potential source of conflict and controversy (Zips, 2000).

This conflict may partly be avoided by the claimed and reported financial commitment of Bobo artists to provide the Order with one tenth of their earnings (Zips, 2006; Kamimoto, 2015, p. 45) that is being *used for preparatory steps towards mass repatriaton and the building of EAIBC branches in Africa* (Zips, 2006, p. 157). Positioned in a strong and militant stance of rejection of the capitalist system, any participation of the Bobo Shanti Order in the monetary system outside the ones assigned to them and authorized by King Emmanuel I (Kamimoto, 2015) is somehow doomed to carry traces of paradox behavior. With the Honorable Priest Henry disclosing his conviction that according to Bobo teachings the skin of Black babies is being processed and used as a resource to produce paper money one might assume that any type of monetary activity would be critically scrutinized and evaluated. On the other hand, the same Honorable Priest Henry noted – not without pride – that he is running a small spare car parts business from out of his humble housing at the compound, while nearby villagers reported regular visits of delegations of Jamaican elders from the Order's headquarter in Bull Bay in big and luxurious four-wheel drives.

E) Moral superiority, dietary approach and attitude towards drugs

Let me tell you dis
We got no filthy, dirty appetite
Quit your low down ways and city lifestyle

Rasta Set The Trend (Lutan Fyah, 1998c)

Being labeled as *a highly organized and disciplined house* (Chevannes, 1994, p. 68) among the various Rastafarian branches, it does not come as a surprise that the Bobo Shanti draw a big part of their identity from their strict adherence to the established rules and regulations, as demonstrated by Sizzla's *Mash Dem Down* (Sizzla, 2002c):

Cyah dis di Rastaman because him on his foundation rigid
Love and righteousness is with di youths govern the village
All dem gwan like dem bad and dem wicked
King Selassie govern the earth, so don't be stupid

Therefore, attempts of distinguishing themselves from the *pagans* by establishing a dichotomy of clean and dirty is a frequent pattern in Bobo lyrics, with their militant – and yet symbolic, in the sense of *word, power and sound* – stance on how to deal with these *pagans* as a main source for them being labeled as religious radicals (Sizzla, 2002c):

Ah, just like in the older days
Chop off the Pagan head and let it roll away
Listen to what I got to say
Praise the king everyday

However, unlike most Roots Reggae singers and hardly backed by Bobo guidelines of conduct and occupation, artists like Sizzla defend what could be seen as a conflicting lifestyle from the outside by stressing that they *make money* and enjoy music but still stick to core values of *cleanliness* expected by the Order's members on tracks like *Jah Works* (Sizzla, 2004a):

Pagan ask if you see me, say you don't
They do dirty things that I won't
I show love, I make money, damn, can't even count
Me and my girl listen the music and bounce about
Those people think they know my whereabouts
The children and the woman, that's all I care about
They act as if cleanliness, they never hear about

Cleanliness and *righteousness* – represented by the broom and the turban in Bobo symbolism – are two central core values of the Order that are most frequently referred to in order to constitute their claim of moral superiority in regard to the *heathens*, who do not participate in Bible-based Bobo practices such as the honoring of *the Sabbath*, as furthermore demonstrated by Sizzla's *Remember* (Taiyuan, 2008):

Always remember be strong in this time
Heathen rage when the righteous climb
Never let them get you down, keep yuh mind now
Pollute the Sabbath, yuh pollute mankind
Remember be strong in this time

Yet another reference to the most honored day of the Old Testament can be found on *The Only King* (chadwick gillingss, 2014) by Lutan Fyah:

Red, gold, and green, Rastaman paint graffiti
And it is our custom to smoke the Sensi
Ital stew, keep the Sabbath day weekly
(...)
These things Selassie I teach me

On *Be Still* (Sizzla, 2005a), Sizzla is speaking out an invitation to *hold a Sabbath on Bobo Hill* and appeals to *Ghetto Youths* to keep their behavior in line with the Ten Commandments:

Thou shall not kill, be still
Go hold a Sabbath ah Bobo Hill
Manifest Selassie I will, tell dem
Di blood fi stop spill
(...)
Not until we overstand ourselves, blood nuh go stop spill
Ten commandment, keep dem still
Ghetto youths, behave yourself and you save yourself
Rastafari made us and not we of our self

The following lines of *Give Dem Ah Ride* (Sizzla, 1997e) serve to illustrate how the *livety* – the morally superior Bobo lifestyle as set by King Emmanuel I – as well as the Order's settlement *high up on Bobo hill* are presented and promoted as a safe refuge from the drug- and fornication-infested society *down inna Babylon*:

Emmanuel set the livety, it ah lick yuh like sledge
Yuh want principle cuz King Selassie ah di head
Stop snort yuh coke, look how you magga like thread
We see you and the harlot lie down inna bed
Sharin' defilement all with the dead
Uno come ah Bobo hill ghetto youths instead
Cuz down inna Babylon no stop run red

While Bobo artists usually stress their intention to stay away from *wicked* behavior, Five Percenters stick to the group's typical recruitment patterns among deliquents and social outlaws, just like Lord Jamar claimed (Lord Jamar, 2006a): *Supreme Mathematics – this ain't black magic, I do my work amongst dope fiends and crack addicts.* Even if they condemn the use of alcohol and drugs, they would still identify those affected by *reefer* and *liquor* as their main target audience on their mission to teach the ignorant – as indicated by the Poor Righteous Teachers on *Word Iz Life* (Poor Righteous Teachers, 1996a):

I educate you through the teacher in me
There ain't no reefer in me
One swig of malt liquor end a nigga
I touch the mic and universally greet, rising earths with peace
And you know how I'm like that
Do this for Blacks stranded in projects
Cashing welfare checks, we got to do what we gots to

Bobos – due to their less missionary and rather reclusive attitude – usually take a more judgmental and exclusive stance towards *sinners*, since involvement in *wicked behavior* is simply not tolerated among the members of the Order, as demonstrated in *Nuh Cross Mi Line* (Lutan Fyah, 2013) by Lutan Fyah:

No ties with no fu-funky licky-licky bar flies
Mi nuh let dem inna mi life
Striptease gwaan across di road but mi nuh tek off mi clothes

Frequently, the judgment of the Bobos is based on religious authority or Biblical sources and *Scribes and Pharisees* are being incorporated as a reference to contemporary *dutty lifestyle*, defined as *skylarks in the street, flirt in the towns* – commited by those who trod on *the ungodly path,* how Sizzla put it in *Good Ways* (Sizzla, 1998e):

Yuh see the dutty lifestyle, the Rastaman ah bun it
(...)
They not different from those
Scribes and Pharisees who come around
They lurks in the corners
Skylarks in the street, flirt in the towns
(...)
Say dem better, so them ah close in
Contempt the youth them whey they pass
Every man is equal
Rastafari say trod not on the ungodly path

Victimized youths, affected by drug habits, are presented with *cleanliness* as the main thing to avoid falling into the traps of systemized destruction on Sizzla's *You World Leaders* (Sizzla, 2004b):

Cocaine is damaging, how the children managin'
So then you try stoppin' him, addicted it has gotten him?
What the fuck is up with him, why the cops shottin' him?
How you taggin' him, why you flatten him?
All because of system, I won't be no victim
Cleanliness is the main thing, one blessed king and sing

In *Open Up The Doors* (Sizzla, 2009), Sizzla is addressing a warning to the Mosaic Pharaoh in a re-contextualization of the imperial forces of contemporary times as well as asking the *Most High* to protect him from *the wicked* and their alcohol, the *illegal liquid*, since – as he further claims on another occasion – *Only Jah and Jah alone, can protect us from the filthyness and wickedness around* (Sizzla, 2007b).

Pharaoh, Pharaoh, Pharaoh... beware yaw
Most High protect I from the wicked
Most High protect I from illegal liquid
Most High provided oxygen and liquid
Most High Selassie I make us rigid
(...)
We got to know that the holy, holy, holyah
Sabbath we gotta keep it
Beat Nyahbinghi drum, beat Nyahbinghi drum
Day and night we seh fi beat it

Interestingly enough, during the field research at the Bobo Shanti settlement in Koforidua, the Priests were frequently engaging in the drinking of palm wine, that does not seem to fall in that category obviously. Kitzinger (1969) obtained similar ethnographic informations when she was assured that they would use it for medical purposes only and it *would not make a man drunk because it was so pure* (p. 247). On the other hand, rappers like the Wu-Tang Clan have caused controversy within the Five Percenters for promoting an image that associates the ideology with drugs, alcohol

(Swedenburg, 1996, p. 8), crime and the objectification of women (Knight, 2013, p. 216). A rather sensitive issue, that also has been raised by Knight (2013, p. 182) in the course of his research:

> *There are many pictures to paint in hip-hop, the Wu-Tang's Raekwon told me, and the Wu paints them all.*

However, there is a clear similarity to the hybrid identity of Dancehall-Rastas like Sizzla or Turbulence who seem to switch between the Old Testament and their new girlfriend in their artistic output without hesitation and successfully cater to different crowds, as illustrated earlier. Not unlikely, Gosa (2011, p. 5) accentuated the eclectic character of Hip Hop music and culture and suggested the intended construction of a rather functional combination of contrasting elements. It can be assumed that Hip Hop as a culture as well as a musical style is highly eclectic in itself and contrasting patterns presented in rap lyrics might as well be attributed to its hybridist construction as political and entertainment, situated *at the junction of entertainment and calculated identity politics* (p. 5).

One might assume that artists are very well aware about the fact that they are actually dealing with two different audiences – that might be labeled as either commercial and ignorant about the deeper meanings or cultural and equipped with the literacy to decode these meanings in turn. In the words of Wu-Tang's Masta Killa on *Triumph* (Wu-Tang Clan, 1997b) – while *The dumb are mostly intrigued by the drum*, the Five Percenter doctrine passed on over the music bears the subversive potential for *Givin sight to the blind*:

Ninety-three million miles away from
Came one to represent the Nation
This is a gathering of the masses
That come to pay respects to the Wu-Tang Clan
As we engage in battle, the crowd now screams in rage
The High Chief, Jamel Irief, take da stage

Light is provided through sparks of energy
From the mind that travels in rhyme form
Givin sight to the blind
The dumb are mostly intrigued by the drum

Another example that serves to underline the possible awareness of performing the role of the preacher and the entertainer at the same time can be found on Brand Nubian's aptly titled *Dance To My Ministry* (Brand Nubian, 1990d), with rapper Lord Jamar claiming to *speak the truth from the DJ booth*:

You find I speak the truth
From the DJ booth, straight to the youth of the inner city
And the outskirts, some may disagree but yo hey, the truth hurts
Lord Jamar and I'll advance in the industry
I'm makin' sure you can dance to my ministry

In contrast to the considerable number of Five Percenters who do not codemn the consumption of drugs and alcohol, as well as several other Rasta branches such as the Twelve Tribes, the use of marijuana in the Bobo Shanti community is restricted to sacral purposes in regular worshipping ceremonies. However, participation in the consumption of the drug is no requirement for being allowed to take part in communal ceremonies. According to the Honorable Priest Henry, smoking marijuana in public is not encouraged in the Bobo Shanti Rastafari Mansion, since it is seen as a spiritual rite that is limited to periods of worship.

Nevertheless, Bobo-affiliated artists such as Anthony B., Capleton, Sizzla, Lutan Fyah, Turbulence or Jah Mason frequently refer to the drug and smoke it on stage or in videos. However, the use of the drug on the compound is prohibited on the day of the Sabbath, when Bobos hold a fast that would usually be broken with a morsel of bread at sunset (Zips, 2006, p. 141). Although Knight (2013) has mentioned the occurrence of fasting periods among Five Percenters, they would be of clearly different nature and consist of a rather odd nutritional diet limited to ice cream and water over the period of a week

(p. 132) that Wu-Tang's Ghostface Killah might refer to on *Wildflower* (Ghostface Killah, 1996a):

I'm the first nigga that had you watching flicks by DeNiro
You gained crazy points, baby, just being with God
Taught you how to eat the right foods, fast, and don't eat lard
I gave you earth lessons, I came to you as a blessing
You didn't do the knowledge what the God was manifesting

In his comparative study of Rastafarian movements and the Nation of Islam, Barnett (2006, p. 877) pointed out that (t)*he articulation that God has manifested himself in the flesh here on Earth is perhaps the key and most enduring similarity between both groups*, referring to the matter that Emperor Haile Selassie I and Fard Muhammad are both revered as the manifestation of *God in the flesh* by Rastafarians and followers of the Nation of Islam alike. However, the same conception can be found in the context of Five Percent Nation founder *Father Allah* Clarence 13X Smith as well as King Emmanuel I Charles Edwards – that Bobos refer to as the *Black Christ in Flesh*.

> (...) *what follows from the corresponding conception of the 'Divinity of Man' is that the human body is the temple of God; and therefore, one should take great care of it. As a result, both movements advocate a healthy diet that serves to maintain the physical body as best as is possible...* (Barnett, 2006, p. 877).

In *Break I Down* (Lutan Fyah, 2011c), Bobo artist Lutan Fyah is making the connection between divine energy and physical health – achieved through vegetarian diet and essential oils – as follows:

Di love of Selassie I affection is so real
Give I di vision inna every faculty
Vitalize, give I strength and energy
Life power keep breath inna mi body
Most High power is like vitamin and enzymes
Vegetables and essentail oils –

Clean mi bloodstreams and renew my mind
Maintain mi hormones, not a negative sign

Brand Nubian's Lord Jamar is suggesting a similar perspective on *Drop The Bomb* (Brand Nubian, 1990b), presenting a rather elitist conception regarding the crucial influence of nutrition and fasting rites on sprituaI health and growth according to Percenter doctrine:

Why do we fear, the devil now that he's a grown man
'cause he bought you, taught you how to eat the wrong food
But now it's time for fasting
Life everlasting, offer thy I-Self
Lord and Master and all things in my circumference
Lord Jamar makes a difference
I have no tolerance for Black ignorance
I keep striving, driving 'cause I'm driven
By the course of Allah, the true and living
Cream of the planet earth, God of the Universe
The first soul, Black like coal

The most frequent references to righteous diet in Five Percenter Rap are concerned with the condemnation of pork, as is the case with the Poor Righteous Teachers – one of the most visible and declared Five Pecenter Rap outfits from the early 1990s. On *Gods, Earths And 85ers* (Poor Righteous Teachers, 1996b) – similar to Rasta ideology and the above quoted lines from Lutan Fyah – the avoidance of pork meat is attributed with longer living and seen as integral part of a proper lifestyle, in accordance with Five Percenter interpretations:

Teach, add on to the life that we live
God degree, twelve jewels, eat the food that I give
No pig, strictly kosher mathematics and fact
Poor Blacks on track mission to take the earth back
(...)
Come get your cash, fill your mind with swine and dash
For longevity, these niggas we will never be

This severe shunning of pork meat provides a common ideological pattern between Five Percenters and Bobos and can be found in corresponding articulations expressed in the output of the artists affiliated with the two groups. As pointed out by Pollard (1982, p. 36):

> *The serious Rastafarian rejects meat and eats only I-tal food which consists chiefly of vegetables. Pork, despised beyond the level of other meat becomes 'dat' (that) a thing to point at, not to touch.*

As illustrated by the following lines of Capleton on *Bun Dung Dreddie* (Capleton, 2000), the consumption of pork – together with the use of drugs – is considered as being *hang up inna John Paul rope,* in the sense of falling victim to the traps of the oppressive colonial power, symbolically personified as the head of the Catholic Church:

How you fi Ras and then you still ah eat pork
How you fi Ras and then you still ah smoke coke
Still all ah sail pon Babylon boat
(...)
Nuff ah tek heroine and nuff ah tek coke
(...)
Nuff ah dem ah hang up inna John Paul rope

A similar pattern can be observed in *Ain't No Mystery* (Brand Nubian, 1993a) by Brand Nubian – with the culmination of *eatin swine, cheap wine* and the *welfare line* indicating an identical criticism, that is defining the instruments of oppression forced on the victims of what has been referred to as internal colonialism (Blauner, 1969), together with the afterlife-orientation of the Christian belief, as a systematic trap to hinder the realization of the *true and living God* in every Black man:

Allah's god, always has been always will be
Never could be, a fuckin' mystery
But you pray for Jehovah to come
That'll be the day when you leave the slum
Until that time, you just keep eatin' swine
Drinkin' cheap wine on the welfare line

The avoidance of salt as part of the Rastafarian dietry restrictions as they are practiced among the Bobos in Koforidua on the other hand does not provoke much mentioning in the music of artists related to the Order. Although it could be explained as a neglectable topic at first hand, the salt taboo bears a rather strong metaphysical meaning in itself that is closely linked to African origins as well (Warner-Lewis, 1993, p. 115):

> *Could one equote salt here with earthly life? Salt-avoidance would therefore connote intense spirituality and would equate with orthodox Rastafari avoidance of political, financial and other wordly preoccupations. This equation of spiritual power and salt-avoidance explains the practice of excluding salt from ancestral offerings of cooked food.*

Next to echoing African religious rituals, the salt taboo bears another dimension in itself, that might be traced back to the slave period and a corresponding myth *that slaves who had not eaten salt were able to fly back to Guinea* (Warner-Lewis, 1993, p. 115) – with the central topic to return to their African home resurfacing in the attempts of repatriation in Rastafari philosophy.

F) Attitude towards gender and homosexuality

> *Blue for boys, pink for girls, girls for boys, boys for girls*
> *Red, gold and green rule the world*
>
> Move Up (Sizzla, 2004c)

By attesting *patriarchal conservative positions on gender relations* (Barnett, 2006, p. 879) as common points between the Nation of Islam and Rastafarian groups, Barnett offers an explanation for the vigorous rejection of homosexuality that Five Percenters and Bobos have been criticized for:

> *As such, both movements castigate homosexuality based on it being considered immoral, ungodly, and forbidden by the Bible and the Quran. Great emphasis also is placed on gender roles within the family, with the woman as the primary caretaker of the children and the house, and the man as the provider.*

The role of the woman has undergone considerable changes since the rise of the Rastafarian belief in the 1930s without a doubt (Rowe, 1980; Turner, 1991; Julien, 2003; Tutturen Nilsson, 2013). Although treated with official respect and addressed as *Royal Princess* or *Empress*, the Bobo Shanti woman is still considered as potentially contaminating the purity of the Priests, in direct analogy to the Biblical Eve, as described by Chevannes (1994, p. 179). His consideration of the Bobo Shanti as the most restrictive of all Rasta Mansions in regard to dealing with its female members is corresponding to the following observations of Zips (2006, p. 142).

> *Other Rastafari houses and individuals keep as well certain taboos around the female menstruation cycle, but none of these come even close to the separation of each woman in the Bobo Ashanti commune in the 'sick house'.*

The woman is basically expected to spend her time isolated in the *sick house* during a considered period of impurity that is being calculated for covering twenty-one days of the month. For this duration of impurity, she is as well excluded from ceremonial gatherings on the Sabbath, since – together with the twenty-one day principle of purification – these practices are being considered *as ancient principles before the beginning of slavery* (Zips, 2006, p. 141).

> *A woman is only allowed to take part in the sabbath ceremonies (inside the tabernacle), if she is ritually pure according to the female taboos set up by King Emmanuel. Even then, man and women don't sit side by side, but are divided into the left male side in the tabernacle and the female right side.*(ibid.)

However, as pointed out by Warner-Lewis (1993), these rather severe restrictions can be traced back to origins in religious traditions practiced by ancient African tribes and their perception of motherhood as the primary spiritual characteristic of women, therefore, *it is the physiological and metabolic attributes that empower motherhood which justify the ostracism of women during menstruation and location* (pp. 118-119):

> *Their spiritual energies are now considered low since the body fluids which are life-giving are being drained away. In these conditions, women are considered contaminants. Thus, among the Nyasa, menstruating women are interdicted from touching salt; elsewhere in Africa, as it is also among the Bobo sect of Rastafari in Jamaica, such women must remain confined to their enclosure* (ibid.).

Adherence to Bobo doctrine among affiliated artists in that matter can be observed in the tendency that women are strongly appreciated and honored in their role as mothers, as reflected in Lutan Fyah's *Mama Love* (Lutan Fyah, 2014), *Mama Don't Cry* (Lutan Fyah, 2011d) or *Don't Make Mama Bawl* (Lutan Fyah, 2012), Jah Mason's *Mother* (Chaîne de yerpee, 2008) and *Mama* (Jah Mason, 2010), as well as Junior Reid's *Love Mama* (Junior Reid, 2007), Sizzla's *Thank U Mama* (Sizzla, 2002d), *Greatest Mother*

(Krish Genius Music, 2016), *Mama Pain* (Realest Entertainment, 2014), *Black Woman And Child* (Sizzla, 1997f), or the following excerpt from *Hot Like Fire* (Sizzla, 2006):

Biggin' up da girls, we are lifting up da girls
Let them know they're the mothers of the earth

A similar pattern can be observed among Five Percenter artists such as Wu-Tang's Ghostface Killah on tracks like *All That I Got Is You* (Ghostface Killah, 1996b) – a touchy ode to his mother that hardly manages to balance his sexist and misogynous portrayal of women throughout the rest of the album (Ghostface Killah, 1996c). However, the estimation of Bobo women as being affected by the most extreme form of subordination among all the different Rastafarian branches is furthermore illustrated by the consideration of even male children – the potential *'King-man' or 'God-man'* (Chevannes, 1994, p. 176) – as being superior to all females. Sizzla's declaration that the *lifestyle of the woman has to be pure and clean* (Sizzla, 1998a) can be considered as the normative conception among the Bobo Shanti. Similarly – and in contrast to their male, *divine* counterparts – Five Percenter women are referred to as Muslims, since they are supposed to bear witness to their husbands being *Gods* – the same way that orthodox Muslims bear witness to Allah (Nuruddin, 2006, p. 128) – in accordance to Five Percenter doctrine that claims that *only a man can achieve the level of perfection symbolized by a 7, whereas a woman can only reach a 6* (Swedenburg, 1996, p. 8). Furthermore, both groups share a similar position towards the need of the women in their community to conceal themselves, as demonstrated by the following lines of Sizzla – who identifies a lack of knowledge about their royal Ethiopian descendance as the reason for them to expose themselves:

Fi ya woman today, look pon whey yuh practice
Yuh nah make no love yet you expose nakedness
For you no see yuhself as Ethiopian...

Sizzla – who on *Pure & Clean* (Sizzla, 1998a) proclaims that *life of the woman has to be pure and clean* – has addressed the responsibility of men to not encourage improper behavior among women in *Lift Mine Eyes* (Sizzla, 2000c) and encouraged the latter to visit the Bobo headquarters on Zion Hill – given that they put on a *tall skirt*:

Young man, don't make the young woman flirt
Mt. Zion a call, so wear you tall skirt

In the following lines of *I.S.L.A.M.* (Lord Jamar, 2006c), Lord Jamar is suggesting the expected dress code and moral superiority of Five Percenter women – referred to as *Earths* in Percenter symbolism and terminology – that have to cover three fourths of their body, in accordance to water covering three fourths of the planet (Swedenborg, 1997, p. 8):

Sweep the devil off the earth, like spring clean
My earth's rock 3/4's, never bring jeans
I be the All Eye Seeing, Supreme Being

Nevertheless, members of the Wu-Tang Clan are among the most criticized Hip Hop artists in regard to expressing misogynous tendencies in their lyrics, with Ghostface Killah's *Wildflower* (Ghostface Killah, 1996a) often being cited in that context. However, the seemingly controversial lyrics ask for a deeper analysis in the light of Five Percenter knowledge, as suggested by Knight (2013, p. 216), since the rapper *expresses a paradoxical view toward Earths: in his role as God, he takes responsibility to civilize woman, but also rebukes her with sexually degrading language*. He furthermore put attention to the point, that this ambivalent approach is a constant factor in the creative output of the Wu-Tang Clan, which would fit into the pattern of serving educational and entertainment purposes that hinder the construction of a single, consistent identity to be personified by the artists (p. 217):

> A rejection of the attitudes in 'Wildflower' can be found elsewhere in the Wu-Tang's body of work. 'Wu Revolution' begins with Ol' Dirty Bastard decrying misogyny as part of the 'mental death' from which the NGE offers resurrection.

Brand Nubian's *Sincerely* (Brand Nubian, 1998b) – offering a truly royal treatment of the *Earths* and praisal of the virtuous Black woman – and the degrading content of *Love Me Or Leave Me Alone* (Brand Nubian, 1993d), addressing females who would not submit to the Five Percenter rules, are but another example of this dichotomy. The same pattern of a conflicting approach towards women can be found combined in one track on Capleton's *Pure Woman* (Capleton, 2002):

She press my pants and press mi shirt seh everything neat
She clean mi house and spread mi bed mi get a good sleep
She gimme di food and gimme mi roots so mi can do it sweet
She nah fi bite she nah fi bow dat mean she nah freak
Mi nah box mi nah fi thump dat mean mi nah fi beat
(...)
She a mi queen, she a mi wife, she a mi empress
And she ever step out inna di latest
And she nah fi expose nuh nakedness

One significant difference between female members of Five Percenters and Bobo Shanti in dealing with gender roles is that the former are actively participating in the music industry as recording artists. Considerably successful vocalists like Lady Mecca of Digable Planets, Queen Latifah or Erykah Badu (Swedenburg, 1996, p. 8; McMurray, 2007) serve as role models for a strong and self-confident identity of the *Earths* that is fully absent on the Bobo side of things.

Chi-Chi man could never sit on Rastaman throne
Char dem with words, fire and sound
Pon the wicked heart, we deh go dash brimstone

As demonstrated by the above quoted lines of Sizzla's *Aznaldo* (Sizzla, 1998f), not surprisingly, Bobos and Five Percenters take a similar radical stand when it comes to homosexuality. A vast list of Jamaican music featuring references of explicit violence towards homosexuals or symbolic burning of homosexuals based on Biblical allusions, as well as non-violent – but yet homophobic – songs can be found on the Soulrebels website (Murder inna Dancehall – 'Nuff with da Chi Chi Man songs!, n. d.). Sizzla and Capleton are among the most frequently named artists in all categories, with other Bobos like Junior Reid and Anthony B. being mentioned as well. A perception, that corresponds with the considerations of Gutzmore (2004, p. 130), who sees Capleton as being *responsible for the largest number of such songs, closely rivalled by deejay Beenie Man*, next to several similar claims about a number of songs by Anthony B. (p. 130) and Bobo artist Turbulence, whose hybrid identity is described by Gutzmore as follows (p. 131):

> *He places on view in parts of his work seamlessly stitched together elements from the deejay-created tradition of righteousness, Selassie-laudation, homophobia and hetero/sexism, with a brocade of God-approved and divinely required violence that culminates in the deadly couplet identifying man and woman as the 'perfect pair' followed by an invocation of 'pure gun' the shots from which will 'tear . . . skulls'.*

Although artists like Sizzla have repeatedly been forced to cancel concerts in Europe due to protests by Gay Rights activists (Larcher & Robinson, 2009), Bobo deejays are by far not the only Jamaican artists accused of *gaybashing*. Therefore it has been suggested that the traditional, patrial society of the island might play a bigger role in that than actual affiliation with the Bobo Shanti Order. An article in the LGBT-magazine OUTfront ("What happened to One Love?", 2004) that interviewed the anonymous program manager of J-FLAG (Jamaica Forum for Lesbians, All-Sexuals and Gays) stated that (r)*eligion is an extremely powerful force in Jamaican society* (p. 1). Highlighting the important role of the Christian Church in the struggle for emancipation and education, the respondant furthermore hinted to the widespread fundamentalist interpretation of the Old Testament and the denunciation of homosexuality as a common feature in sermons. Nevertheless, the anonymous program manager specifically referred to the literal interpretation of the Bible by the Bobo Shanti Rastafari denomination and its increasing growth and popularity on the island. A popularity certainly linked to the considerable number of Reggae and Dancehall artists that openly pledge allegiance to the Order and frequently display homophobic references in their lyrics: *Singers such as Capleton, Sizzla and Buju Banton often defend their homophobic lyrics which include incitements to violence against LGBT people, by using their religious teachings as a justification* (p. 1). Referring to a concert of Bobo artists Capleton and Sizzla in St. Elizabeth, Jamaica, in 2004, the article stated that (u)*sing the derogatory terms for gay men "chi-chi-man" or "battybwoys" - they urged the audience to "kill dem, battybwoys haffi dead, gun shots pon dem...who want to see dem dead, put up his hand"* (p. 2). As pointed out by Cooper (2005), the club or dancehall can be characterized as a clearly defined hetero space (p. 1), where not only the sound systems clash, but also intentionally exaggerated interpretations of feminity and masculinity. It has been discussed earlier that homophobia can be seen far from being limited to specific circles in Jamaica, but as a very present pattern, widespread in society (p. 9). However, as noted by Cooper, there is a specific practical aspect to it, that is often overlooked by Western critics judging on the matter (ibid.):

> (...) *Jamaicans are generally socialised to recognise the fact that* anti-homosexuality *values are entirely compatible with knowing acceptance of* homosexuals *within the community. This is a fundamental paradox that illustrates the complexity of the ideological negotiations that are constantly made within the society.*

However, Sizzla responded to the accusations with the non-compromising *Nah Apologize* (Sizzla, 2005b), in which he also raised the issue of being judged from an outside perspective by critics unfamiliar with Jamaican society and culture:

Some bwoy bow down...bow down doing what?
Nothing in the world could ever have me doing that
I don care if they ban me, damn me
Say, fi bun batty-man you cyah wrong me
Yow, me no born over England
A real African dis, real Rastaman dis

Despite the fact that homophobia is present throughout different social classes – and might be *conceived as an articulation of an Africanist world-view in which the essential complementary of opposites is affirmed* (Cooper, 2005, p. 9) – the rather frequent acts of physical violence against homosexuals are *usually restricted to working-class communities where hierarchies of impoverishment and marginalisation are institutionalized* (p. 9). However, on a more sophisticated level, carefully placed hints about the possible homosexuality of the political competitor are being instrumetalized to discredit the target among voters – as in the case of Prime Minister Patterson during the 2001 elections (p. 10).

The adaption of an anti gay song – *Chi Chi Man* by TOK (TOK, 2001) – as a political anthem in order to raise questions about the sexual orientation of the competing candidate expressed but one side of the story. Nevertheless, (t)*he fact that Patterson's party still won the elections might, however, be proof that the accepted nationalist narrative might not be as uncontested as one might presume* (Davis, 2006, p. 27). Or, as furthermore argued, while *reggae and dancehall have become part of a global black cultural discourse of resistance and counter-identity* (p. 24), for Jamaicans it embodies *the morals and values of 'home' as expressed by yardies, whose national loyalty identifies them as the ultimate signifiers of a Jamaican identity that can stand in opposition to the corruption of Western materialism* (ibid.). Davis (p. 25) further concluded that:

> (...) *within Jamaican society the clearest embodiment of the difference that 'corrupts' and 'contaminates' national identity is the homosexual. Seen as antiethical to national development and disruptive of social harmony, the homosexual stands as an accepted sign of external, western corruption-a result of Babylon's moral decay and degeneracy.*

In consequence, this perspective calls for the construction of a counter identity, defined by hightened masculinity (Davis, 2006, p. 25):

> *The yardie, as the 'true Jamaican', is carefully constructed in opposition to the homosexual as non-citizen and comes to embody the sign of a rigidly gendered and oppressively heterosexual nation.*

Anderson and McLean (2014) have dealt at lengths with the dramatized and widespread phenomenon of Shibboleth in Jamaican language – with any mentionings that could bear references to homosexuality radically being deleted from one's vocabulary in order to not leave the slightest doubt about the unquestionable heterosexual identity and masculinity of the speaker. Next to the number *Two* being avoided and replaced by *second* or *twice*, *Manchester* would turn into *Gyalchester* in order to signalize preference of females over males and even *menu* turns to *gyalu* for the same reason. What might seem quite exaggerated and ridiculous to some can become crucial to others, who live in a surrounding in which two men are stoned for being spotted next to each other with the respective numbers Six and Nine printed on the back of their football jerseys (2014, p. 34). Stemming from the strong rejection of oral sex practices derived from interpretations of Rastafarian philosophy and Christian religion as the possibly strongest ideological influences on Jamaican society – such pointless acts of violence bear strong resemblance to the infamous turf wars between *Bloods* and *Crips* in Los Angeles – where people would get killed for wearing red or blue on the wrong side of the street and a similar strategy to wipe out any trace of the rivaling gang in speech and act is being used (2014, p. 32).

However, this solution of *linguistic avoidance* applied by Jamaicans might serve as yet another explanation for the frequent gaybashing in the output of Bobo artists, that puts it in perspective of a bigger social context of problematic developments. To a certain degree, it furthermore relativates the criticized *fyah bun* rhetorics, since Anderson and McLean quote one of their informers describing the purpose of Shibboleth as (d)*i man dem a try bun out everyting weh allude to dat* [*men are trying to condemn everything related to it*] (Anderson & McLean, 2014, p. 25). It is noteworthy that Cooper (2005, p. 20) also suggested that homosexuality is often perceived to be linked to pedophilia as well – which is partly responsible for the strong rejective stance of Jamaicans on the issue. Referring to Bobo artists like Sizzla, Capleton or Anthony B. – who introduced a enhanced radical rhetoric of intolerance articulated within existing Rasta ideology in Dancehall –, Davis (2006) connotates the use of the seemingly impulsive and unreflected use of the 'fire' term with a more complex meaning in the context of identity building, arguing that (d)*ancehall's new 'prophets' positioned the metaphor of fire and the theme of cleansing as integral parts of the project of cultural and national reclamation* (p. 26). Capleton's interpretation of that project has been captured by Davis in the following lines (p. 27):

> *According to Capleton, 'the healing of the nation is the primary project. But increasingly it is the homosexual who is seen as antiethical to the nation's health. In his song 'Bun Di Chi Chi,', Capleton employs both the metaphors of blood and fire in the call to cleanse the 'inequity' of the 'chi chi'...*

Davis (2006, p. 27) futher argued *that many songs in dancehall, like Sizzla's 'Pump Up,' express hostility toward gay men as a part of a wider celebration of black female sexuality,* what therefore marks the extent to which anti-gay sentiment is not only normalized but is used to fix social relationships – a sort of *rally 'round the flag* on the cost of stigmatizing a specific social group. The following is Davis' attempt to establish a historical link between this pattern and the social structures shaped by the slave trade era (p. 27):

> *In Caribbean slave societies, hegemonic masculinity ensured its own power primarily through the control of black bodies. White heterosexual males at the apex of society positioned themselves not only as economically and politically powerful, but also exercised ultimate sexual control over women's bodies and physical control over black male bodies.*

As a consequence, he concluded that (b)*y stripping black men of rational power, black masculinities could simultaneously be feminised and dismissed as infantile* (Davis, 2006, p. 28). As pointed out by Cheney (1999, p. 2), movements linked to Black Nationalism usually share the primal purpose of rehabilitating Black manhood. Although often overemphasized and out of proportion, these strategies can be seen as a rational response to an irrational experience (p. 3). A central aspect is the need for a clearly defined power center that serves as an influential source for the construction of new, empowered identities. This power center can be identified easily as Haile Selassie I in the case of the Rastafari philosophy – in addition with Black nationalist Marcus Garvey and King Emmanuel I for the Bobo Shanti denomination. Just as these defined power centers are all derived from the Bible as an established source of authenticity and authority, Bobo artists frequently ground and justify their homophobic position by referring to the undisputable *Book of Books*. Although sharing it as the same source of reference with the Christian faith, preachers are being attacked for not being strict enough in their judgment on homosexuals and accused to *defend di slackness* in Sizzla's *Praise Yeh Jah* (Sizzla, 1997g):

I see Bob Marley rise, an unu kill de prophet
Why yuh don't kill those, standing on yuh pulpits
Yuh use dem to steer di minds of di youth
An as dey preach, di youth cease from knowing di truth
Dis is the truth above our circumstances
I see how yuh constantly building churches
But while yuh church defend di slackness as usual
Rasta no mix up with homo

As yet another example for that, *Cyaah Gwaan To Rhatid* (Lutan Fyah, 2015b) shows Lutan Fyah judging *wit di Bible inna mi hand* in regard to structural enforcements of gay liberation – *'cause Christ never make such law*:

> (...) *Things are changing*
> *And a lot a things that papa, mama preached against*
> *Dem a force mi fi tolerate it*
> (...)
> *Say that cyaah gwaan to rhatid*
> *Mi a judge wit di Bible inna mi hand*
> (...)
> *Before parents said it, so make it stay like dat*
> *Jah Jah ten commondements, we obey like dat*
> (...)
> *Hey,they want we tolerate the funny but we tell dem nuh*
> *'cause Christ never make such law*

Homosexuals are frequently referred to as *funny*, as in Bobo artist Junior Reid's *Funny Man* (VISAO3, 2009), featuring another Biblical allusion – *in sunday school they teach us 'bout Adam and Eve, they never teach us 'bout Adam and Steve/certain things just make my heart grieve and my eyes just can't believe*. As a matter of fact, Pinn (2007, p. 293) has questioned the different frame of reference in judging the respective statements of rappers criticized for homophobic and misogynous lyrics and established Biblical sources on the other hand:

> *The sexism expressed by Saint Paul and other biblical figures, the homophobia that marks both testaments has not resulted in a huge theological backlash requiring the destruction of the Bible as a viable 'sacred' text. Why not excercise the same hermeneutic of multiple meanings to rap lyrics and their creators?*

Pinn furthermore hinted towards suggested inconsistencies between the formal theological statements uttered in the context of religious proclamations and its practical implementation in a broader social – or artistic – context (Pinn, 2007, p. 293):

> *This is not to say these artists should not be held accountable, should not be critiqued with regard to behavior and opinions. It simply means recognizing the often problematic relationship between theological pronouncements and arguments and practice that plagues the history of religion in and outside hip hop culture.*

However, further evidence of Biblical legitimation can be found in Sizzla's *Nuh Apologize* (Sizzla, 2005b), where reference is made to the severe punishments foreseen in the *Book of Books* and practiced *inna de Biblical days*:

Damn, it's the lyrical phase, this alone mek dem fret
Inna de Biblical days we use to stone dem to death (...)
Yaw, go and read yuh Bible and read Leviticus
Yuh live in a clean land, then yuh can live with us
What dey say dey do, try to ban me from the UK
Motherfuckers, I'm from Ethiopia, Africa, yaw, straight to Zimbabwe

Brand Nubian – as one of the most visible messengers of Five Percenter doctrine – faced similar accusations as Sizzla or Capleton for the following lines of their hit single *Punks Jump Up To Get Beat Down* (Brand Nubian, 1992):

So I gotta show Dukes the macho lot that I am
I can rock a jam and make the world drop ham
Oh yes, I'm the bad man, and bad men wear black
And if it comes to droppin' bombs, yo, I'm down with that
Though I can freak the fly flow, fuck up a faggot
Don't understand their ways, I ain't down with gays

Unlike the Bobo artists – who turn to their religious doctrine to justify their radical views – Sadat X showed considerable efforts to relativate his choice of words, but mentions deeply rooted homophobic tendencies within the Black community (Constantine-Simms, 2001) in general as well (Rausch, 2011, p. 148):

> (...) *that was a term we used for somebody who was soft. Anyone who was soft was a faggot. And "Don't understand their ways, I ain't down with gays..." At that point and time when we were making that record (...) homosexuality wasn't that out in the open as it is now. Especially in the black community, where that was seen as being taboo. (...) It really wasn't along the lines of us not liking gays.*

However, the official Five Percenter point of view on the issue proofs to be less compromising (Knight, 2013, p. 222). When Five Percent Nation researcher and former member Michael Muhammed Knight got expelled for criticizing Lord Jamar's homophobic track (djvlad, 2013) against Kayne West (Killmann, 2014), the movement's official representative Born Justice Allah confirmed that there is no place for homosexuals among the Nation of the Gods and Earth in an interview with the influential Hip Hop magazine *The Source* (Pologod, 2104). Although there are more and more homosexuals participating in Rap and Hip Hop culture (Chiu, 2005; Wilson, 2007; Means Coleman, R. R. & Cobb, J., 2007), homophobic lyrics probably became even more common since the early 1990s (Hill, 2009; Shimeles, 2010; Berggren, 2012), with words like *fag* or *bitch* being used to degrade imaginary opponents in the context of the competition-oriented art of Rap, as in Wu-Tang's *It's Yourz* (Wu-Tang Clan, 1997c):

Stop the fader of the RAM, blast more watts through my pre-amp
Them can't stress the beat vamp, the shit'll get blamp
At full throttle, hot lead propels throughout my nozzle
Crack your soul like bottles, leave you stiff as models
You fag, you couldn't pull one drag off my blunt
You couldn't punch your way out of a wet paper bag
With scissors in your hands, bitch, the RZA
I stand close to walls like number four the lizard
Enchant a few solar panels, blast off like Roman candles
Rap vandals, stomp your ass like Wahoo McDaniel
You cocker spaniel dogs can't fuck with our catalog
Put your lights out and leave your brain inside a fog

Despite of all that, neither in the case of the Bobo artists, nor in the one of the Five Percenter rappers, homophobia is significantly more widespread than among nonaffiliated musicians in the respective genre (Swedenburg, 1996, p. 9). Therefore, the religious factor can only serve as a limited explanation for these discriminative tendencies, among other influences of socio-cultural origin. Finally, one can not expect the *good Christians* – that centuries of missionary activities were aiming to create – would turn into open minded liberals without a considerable phase of transition (La Font, 2009, p. 115; Bax, 2010). However, while artists like the Wu-Tang Clan actively support AIDS benefits sponsored by gay organizations with appearances at charity shows (Swedenburg, 1996, p. 9; Knight, 2013, p. 209), Bobo artists like Sizzla are more uncompromising in their Mosaic values and heavily involved in constant battles with gay rights movements or the *Stop Murder Music* campaign (SMM) against violent lyrical content (Larcher & Robinson, 2009; Wahab, 2016).

From Mecca to Zion, from Priest to God:
Lost children and hybrid identities

Why settle with being a Priest when you can be a God? Although a certain number of quite striking similarities of Bobos and Five Percenters in regard to dogmatic conception and symbolism have been detected, it would still appear as rather surprising to imagine both ideologies personified by one individual at the same time. Despite the fact that the phenomenon of Muslim Rastas is not necessarily a new one (Savishinsky, 1994b; Soares, 2010; Zips, 2016), their full acceptance is equally disputed among both of the groups they claim to belong to. Declared Five Percenters like Brand Nubian happened to incorporate typical Rasta-related issues such as repatriation on a song called *Black Star Line* (Brand Nubian, 1993e) – in reference to Marcus Garvey's shipping line that was supposed to put the Universal Negro Improvement Association's aim of transferring Black Americans back to Africa into practice in the early twentieth century. However, these historical events tend to serve as a common topic in Reggae-related music – as can be seen by Sizzla's slight update of the theme in *Black Star Airline* (Sizzla, 2013c), for instance. However, a case like this has to be considered as a more general reference to one of the most influential figures involved in Black empowerment strategies who is far from being exclusively referred to in Bobo Shanti doctrine.

Although declared Bobo- and Five Percenter-artists have collaborated before – as in the case of Capleton and Wu-Tang's Method Man on *Wings Of The Morning* (Capleton, 1995) – they did not incorporate elaborated expressions concerning their respective ideological backgrounds at that time. Interestingly enough, one can find both denominations personified in a single individual, the US-based rapper Decipher73i. However, before going deeper into the case of the self-proclaimed Bobo/Percenter it is necessary to pursue a closer investigation of the highly eclectic and esoterically charged rap collective he emerged from, The Lost Children of Babylon. Founded in the mid-1990s, the Philadelphia-based group featuring rappers named Rasul Allah 7 or The

Breath of Judah debuted as guests on a release of the critically acclaimed Jedi Mind Tricks in 1996 (Jedi Mind Tricks, 1996). Being mentored by the controversially discussed Dwight D. York – or Malachi Z. York, Issa Al Haadi Al Mahdi, Dr. York – who got arrested and convicted for child molestation in 2002, The Lost Children of Babylon claim close affiliation with the infamous founder and ideologist of the Nuwaubian Nation – a movement that managed to assert a considerable influence on Hip Hop artists for a while, with big names such as Afrika Bambaataa, Doug E. Fresh, Da Bush Babees, Erykah Badu, Outkast, MF Doom, Posdnuos of De La Soul or Prodigy of Mobb Deep being influenced by the teachings of York (Bibi Khan, 2012).

Formed as a quasi-religious cult that would enhance the already far out conceptions of Black Muslim movements like the Moorish Science Temple, the Nation of Islam or the Five Percenters with elements of UFO-logy, eclectic conspiracy theories and a basic theme of Ancient Egypt in Brooklyn 1967, York even initiated The Lost Children's nominal relocation from *Babylon* to *Egypt* on their second album (The Lost Children of Egypt, 2003) that would extensively explore aspects of Egyptian mythology and philosophy. In the 2000s, the group employed a more politically oriented style that would circulate around conspiracy theories, as displayed on records like *The 911 Report: The Ultimate Conspiracy* (The Lost Children of Babylon, 2006) or *Zeitgeist: The Spirit of the Age* (The Lost Children of Babylon, 2010). With themselves being deeply rooted in a mix of various religions and spiritual concepts, apocalyptic topics, astrology, masonry and conspiracy theories (Nuruddin, 2006), The Lost Children of Babylon developed an extensive franchising practice similar to the one of the Wu-Tang Clan in the late 1990s. Countless offsprings of various artistic quality surfaced, among which Apakalypse, Son of Saturn or the Masta Buildas with their album entitled *Reptilian Body Snatchers* (Masta Buildas, 2009) deserve to be mentioned in regard to demonstrate the broad spectrum of esoteric-religious influences among this circle of artists.

Having defined his actual adventurous artistic and ideological background, it does not really come as a surprise that Decipher73i turns out to be a heavily tattooed rapper wearing uncovered dreadlocks – as where Bobo teaching would condemn the inked skin as a *Bismarck* and ask for a piece of cloth wrapped around the head. Nevertheless, he tried to demonstrate the compatibility of being a Five Percenter and Bobo Shanti by lyrically wrapping up his double personality in songs entitled *Curse Of Allah, Sodom & Gomorrah, Red, Gold & Green* or *Sluts, Hoes & Bitches* on an album entitled *I Of the Heavens* (Decipher73i, 2011). At close inspection the music of Decipher73i turns out to be as ambivalent and eclectic as he himself comes across. Interestingly enough, Washington (2014) aligned a number of artists inspired by the teachings of the Five Percent Nation as well as the Rastafarian faith and linked them both with the ancient concept of divine beings called Raap among West African members of the Wolof tribe. Her considerations are focusing on a common idea of humankind being kept away from the realization of their God-like nature by oppressive forces. A line of thought that she identified in the expressions of Reggae artists like Peter Tosh, Bob Marley or Mutabaruka (p. 85) and declared Five Percenters such as Rakim, Wu-Tang Clan, Gravediggaz and Killarmy alike.

Although the praisal of Haile Selassie as divine majesty or reincarnated Messiah common among Rastas could be identified as being compatible with the Percenters' consideration of Clarence 13X Smith as *Father Allah* and his conception of *man being God*, Washington preferred to somehow connect both lines of thinking by referring to Mutabaruka's demystifying gnostic multifaith approach. The latter is mainly build on the realization of man as the sole and exclusive divine being that can be reached by following different religions – while Wu-Tang's RZA defined religion as relying on something else than your own divine essence. Hence, she concluded that (i)*n the organic holistic worldview of the Five Percent and Mutabaruke [sic], the very concept of religion is anti-ethical and opposed to divinity* (Washington, 2014, p. 86). The problem with this conception is that Mutabaruka is basically an individual thinker and seeker who has developed his very own ideas of spirituality – similar to rapper KRS ONE, who founded The Temple of Hip Hop (KRS ONE, 2009) – that somehow blend in with the heterogenous, gnostic approach of the Five Percenters, but he certainly is not your typical type of Rasta.

Although the doctrinal diversity among various branches of the Rastafarian faith has been argued before (Barnett, 2005) and moderate streams like the Twelve Tribes have been labeled as being *watered-down to a one-love, peace and love, don't worry, be happy, type of organization* (p. 75), it is important to consider that all of them are based on a constitutional religious doctrine that is somehow contrary to the principle of divine self-realization as pursued by the Five Percenters. As laid-back as they might come across, even the Twelve Tribes of Israel – once considered as the most disciplined branch of Rastafari by the time of its formation in 1968 (Tafari, 1995), regular reading of the Bible and acceptance of Haile Selassie as *the Second Coming of Christ*, as well as belief in 144.000 chosen ones to live in the kingdom of God are obligatory (Barnett, 2005, p. 68). The Nyahbinghi Order – also referred to as Theocracy Reign Ancient Order of Nyahbinghi – is thoroughly grounded on the Mosaic law of the Old Testament and requires members to adhere to the vow of the Nazarite mentioned in the Bible (Chakravarty, 2014b). In addition, Bobo Shanti doctrine is strongly based on the Holy Trinity of Prophet, Priest and King – Marcus Garvey, Emmanuel I and Haile Selassie, with Emmanuel considered divine as the reincarnation of Jesus or the *Black Christ in Flesh* (p. 69).

Outlook and discussion:
What's today's mathematics – fyah still ah bun?

Yuh love, yuh no partial
Love for di soldier, di police and di corporal
Dis next generation of youths are not normal
Love and I-nity what how yuh live it royal
I-love in I-ah soul, and the soul is immortal
Don't get mi wrong, mi love my Blackness
But spiritually there is only one exactness
What is immaterial can never be separated and that's a fact

Worldwide Love (Kabaka Pyramid, 2013a)

In the course of the late 1990s and the commercial explosion of Independent Rap – mainly characterized by acts like Company Flow, Cannibal Ox or Deltron 3030 – a considerable amount of intellectual white college rappers flooded the Alternative Rap scene in the pursue of the remarkable Aesop Rock – who has been attested a bigger vocabulary than Shakespeare (Daniels, 2014). In consequence, Black supremacy wrapped up in grimy street tales became one of the things that started to smell funny in the new millenium. After an era characterized by the raised political awareness of visibly militant and influential acts like KRS ONE, Public Enemy or Paris, as well as the quest for meaning in spiritual counter-concepts and -identities outside questioned institutionalized authorities – as personified by commercially successful artists like Brand Nubian, Wu-Tang Clan, Jeru the Damaja or Afu-Ra, that were still able to maintain their street credibility –, the mainstream mood was set to a rather basic party vibe with bumping beats to dance to and simple lyrical content confined to the club. A highly acclaimed and vital independent scene with torchbearers like Immortal Technique that successfully established their own structures remained widely unnoticed by the mass audience on the other hand. While the Five Percent Nation continues to play a significant role in Black American Hip Hop without a doubt, artists tend to remain more low-profile about their affiliation. The self-confident, provocative use of the ideology as proclaimed in the creative output of the Wu-Tang Clan or Brand Nubian during the 1990s has diminished ever since (Knight, 2013, p. 186). However, more recent artists like Hasan Salaam still show tracable elements of Five Percenter ideology in their lyrics, with the following lines from *Kingdom Of Heaven* (Hasan Salaam, 2008a) easily fitting in on anything Brand Nubian recorded three decades ago:

The devil keep us deaf, dumb, and blind
Addicted to crime
Feeding us venomous swine
To poison our minds
(...)
Fact remains that the Sun of Man connot be eclipsed
10% would have you think this living God is a myth

Despite heavy use of Five Percenter vocabulary and conceptions, a clear distinguishing point can be determined by the use of orthodox Islam's central statement – *La illaha ilallah, I bear witness there is none but Allah* – as a repeated hookline for the mentioned song. This eclectic mix of references to various religious and mystical origins – not unlike the earlier discussed case of Decipher73i and The Lost Children of Babylon – continues on a track entitled *Tales Of The Lost Tribe* (Hasan Salaam, 2005a):

Sons of Canaan fabricated ways to enslave us
Willie Lynch tricknology and degrees of the Masons
Black stone shows the origin that Adam was shaped with
They stole our birth rights and replaced it with ways of Pagans
We're the Sun, Crescent Moon and the Star of David
Save the accolades I give Allah all praises
(...)
So rise up mighty nation like the dawn of creation
Put 'em high and grab hold of constellation
Pour some libation for the word and revelation
Allah U Akbar, Ashae, and Amen

With the *Star of David* already being mentioned, Hasan Salaam gets more precise in his respect, embrace and unification of various religious identities, including *Jah* as the Rastafarian divinity:

To the Lost Tribe who questions where Allah is
Or where Jehovah, Yahweh and Jah is
The most high's manifested all around and inside us

Further reference to Rastafarian faith and terminology can be found in the course of his appearance on The REAVERS' – Revolutionary Emcees Advocating their Voices on Everyday Reality's Struggle – track *Warrior* (The Reavers, 2005):

You could consider this the ninety-five theses of Martin Luther
Second shooter from the grassy knoll, virus in your computer
Modern-day Lion of Judah, bring truth from the highest
So the only rock I sling is able to drop Goliath

However, Hasan Salaam keeps on stressing affiliations with orthodox Islam at the same time by referring to *water in the desert straight from Zamzam's well* (Hasan Salaam, 2005a), declaring to brush the dust off his *Holy Qur'an* on *Prayer Of A Sinner* (Hasan Salaam, 2005b), or dedicating a whole song to the day of the central Friday prayer in orthodox Islam on *Jummah* (Hasan Salaam, 2004). Further evidence for the self-depiction of Hasan Salaam as Sunni Muslim is being provided by the opening lines of the aforementioned *Prayer Of A Sinner* (Hasan Salaam, 2005b):

Smoke too many Newports
Plus attend too many court dates to cool off
Been with too many women in sin
Committing too much adultery
Not to have a queen and seed to hold close to me
Been a while since I listened to the Lord when he spoke to me
I just seem to live for today
Was born to decay and don't do my best to pray five times a day
Gotta get saved, but who knows if Allah will forgive my ways

Despite the fact that he collaborated with essential underground artists such as Immortal Technique or Vordul Mega of Cannibal Ox, the impact and visibility of Hasan Salaam and – at their time – highly influential and commercially successful groups like Brand

Nubian, Wu-Tang Clan or Poor Righteous Teachers can in no way be compared. Nevertheless, the pursuance of a less restrictive, more flexible approach in terms of ideology can as well be witnessed among the recent musical voices hailing from Jamaica. Promising new artists around the Zinc Fenc label, such as Kabaka Pyramid, Chronixx, Proteje or Jesse Royal, tend to be affiliated with less strict Rasta branches and follow a more mainstream-oriented approach – while still articulating core Rasta topics that do not lack radical rhetoric, as demonstrated in Chronixx' *Start A Fyah* (ChronixxMusic, 2011):

A no nothing fi mi walk inna Rome
An' start a fyah, start a fyah, yes
A nothing fi mi walk inna Rome
An' start a fyah, mi seh a fyah
Becah dem a ask how a likkle African
A go ignite the whole inna Vatican
But a no nothing fi mi walk inna Rome
Start a fyah, start a fyah

In general, they come across as less separatist, judgmental and offensive as the militant Bobos of the 1990s, with artists like Proteje pursuing a more individual approach of the faith, commenting on the preachy, reclusive nature of the Bobo Shanti and demanding to *Organize and form inna one again* on *I&I* (Proteje, 2013):

Lead who? Dem a lost, we nuh follow dem
Organize and form inna one again
Twelve Tribes, yuh nuh see we with the banner dem
Bobo Hill a talk, walk far, do nuh bother dem
Ithiopia, the Ark of the Covenenant
Queen Makeda, the start of the sovereign
Selassie I order we govering
We nuh inna none a dem tings, so I say

Proteje's labelmate Kabaka Pyramid – although calling to oneness and unity as well – demonstrates a more diplomatic approach in his attempt to *Link Bobo Hill, Orthodox and Twelve Tribe* on *Warrior* (Kabaka Pyramid, 2013b):

Oneness, I and I apply fa
Deep inna meditation mi tek a dive yah
Link Bobo Hill, Orthodox and Twelve Tribe yah
Dem ting deh people fi remind of

Combining a highly individual, spiritually-oriented perspective with sincere respect for the history and heritage of the faith – summed up on *Lead The Way* (Kabaka Pyramid, 2013c) by his lines *Rastaman original, livity so metaphysical, from Bobo Hill straight to Pinnacle* – Kabaka Pyramid elaborates on concepts of religion and spirituality seemingly outside the Rastafarian context by referring to the Kemetic concept (Hilliard, 1985; Nobles, 1986; Hilliard, 1989; Chandler, 2000; Zulu, 2006; Rachell, 2007) and implying a link of the philosophy with ancient Egyptian civilizations on *Liberal Opposer* (Kabaka Pyramid, 2013d):

I am a liberal opposer, practitioner of yoga
Position of the cobra, tradition of the Shona
Trace back my lineage to inna Ethiopia
Down inna Kemet me build di pyramid of Djoser
Hieroglyphics dem a call that Medu Neter
When me see the sun a rise in the sky me call it Kheper
High priest a cure the Leper with praises onto Neter
Them come ya with them cross but mi say the ankh is better
We no want to see no beretta
Rise up fi go take a life up, jus sip the breath of life up
No nyam no flesh and mek sure you exercise nuff
And be careful of the one who teach the Jesus Christ stuff

The rather inclusive approach of Kabaka Pyramid is suggesting that the once as radical, militant and fundamentalist perceived Bobo Shanti interpretation of the Rastafarian philosophy and religion has experienced a more consensual reconsideration among younger artists, who respond to it with rather broad tolerance, acceptance, respect and partly embrace. As an example for the latter case, one might refer to Bugle, who delivers his more moderate and conciliating message of the Order in a much less aggressive musical way than the typical Bobo artist. Despite claims of *mi no simple Rasta, a real Bobo youth/Dem a tell a lie but a wi talk the truth* on *Educated Dunce* (Akam Entertainment, 2014) and hailing *Emmanuel I* on *Survivor* (Krish Genius Music, 2014) in perfect accordance with the characteristic doctrine of the Holy Trinity suggested by the Order, his appearance is much more fashion-oriented and differs strongly from the rather homogenous Bobo dress code – an issue that is picked up in *False Prophet* (unpluggedmm, 2015):

Dem neva si mi wit no turban pon mi head
But man a Bobo same way
Natty Congo still
(...)
Nuff nuff a dem a snake in a lion clothe
Dem a run the church and the hoe houses

The referenced video clip to the song makes heavy use of Bobo Shanti elements, from Priests in robes and turbans beating Nyahbinghi drums to weaving Bobo flags and blazing fire. If he claims that *every Bobo weh si mi seh mi mek dem proud* in *Rasta Party* (Krish Genius Music, 2015), it might be based on his well-dosed but consistent references to the Order, that could be considered as a bridge for those seeking authentic Rastafari knowledge but being turned down by the rather militant reputation of the Bobos, as demonstrated in *Rope* (Bugle, 2015):

Dem say salvation alone last
So mi a tell unno go seek it fast
All who deh yah wah real knowledge
Find yuhself up a Bobo hill college

King Ital Rebel is but another example for that type of artist, that demonstrates a much more Roots Reggae-oriented approach than most of the typical *fire reggae-turbans* and does not fall in the Bobo category by appearance – which does not hinder him from dropping lines like *King Tafari Emmanuel, the truth* and even implying affiliation by stating *Bobo keep it fit, none a dem cyah clown we* on *Jah Warrior* (King Ital Rebel, 2016a). Just like Bugle, King Ital Rebel remains consistent in his referencing of the Order, having a tune called *Emmanuel* and keeping it coming up continuously on *Show Love* (King Ital Rebel, 2016b):

Yes I bless I
Holy Emmanuel Emperor I
InI a give thanks for the breath of life
Emmanuel I
(...)
Equal rights, justice for all
Bobo stand firm, watch di wicked dem fall
Tell Babylon keep dem pork and beans
Bobo keep it balanced, firm and clean

Pressure Buss Pipe – who currently performs as Pressure – is yet another recent artist who presents his audience with an occasional nod towards the Bobo Shanti Mansion. Although being more involved in Bobo symbolism and ideology during his earlier days – including the infamous turban as a headgear – he still refers to the Order's dogmatic principles here and then – such as in *It Haffi Guh Suh* (Pressure, 2011):

Judgment!
Mi seh bun dem like copper, send dem to hell
Dem nah love Blackness, neither Emmanuel

In a certain way, the Bobo-teachings, -identity and -doctrine present themselves to have been merged and incorporated as yet another element to refer to in the canon of established Rastafarian culture, experience and symbolism – which undisputably proves the permanent relevance and consistent role of the Bobo Shanti Rasta Mansion and therefore *burns* the claims of early critics, who deemed it a short trend and temporary nuisance. Somehow, this new generation of artists has internalized the hybrid identity of Bobo artists like Turbulence – who looked at US-Hip Hop for inspiration in music and fashion – and extended it to a more inward-oriented exploration of plurality within the Rastafarian identity. But unlike their counterparts around the millenial turn, it seems to be more natural for them to effortlessly switch between political Conscious Reggae, Roots-oriented Rastafarian content and rather commercial material designated for the Pop- and Rn'B-market – or technically solid raps over hard Hip Hop beats. Kabaka Pyramid even released his first records as a rapper in the style of US-artists before embracing the Rastafarian faith and turning to more local forms of musical expression and is technically capable to compete with any full-time rapper, as demonstrated on *Kabaka vs. Pyramid* (Kabaka Pyramid, 2016), for instance. With commercially successful and critically acclaimed representatives like these, the strong presence of Rastafarian philosophy should be guarranteed in Jamaican popular music for the time being.

While the glorious *age of fire* set ablaze by the wave of Bobo artists in the late 1990s gradually ebbed out and got somehow extinguished by the rise of commercialized Dancehall during the last decade, leading representatives like Sizzla, Capleton or Lutan Fyah are still around and influential. Artists like Mr. Royal or Jah Defender are pursuing the footsteps of Sizzla by combining slack and conscious content in a more edgy approach, catering to the Conscious Reggae as well as the Dancehall crowd. Teflon – who has been referred to as Bobo Shanti music's emerging fire-bearer, next to putting together hardcore Hip Hop albums like *It's Been A Long Time Coming* (Teflon, 2012) – is heavily stressing his affiliation with the Order in songs like *Cleanest Bobo* (Dancehall Seduction, 2014), *Real Bobo, Fyah Is Burning, Burn Dem Out* (Teflon, 2010) or *Man A Bobo* (Teflon, 2008) and prolonguing the tradition of the turbans in Jamaican music:

(...) *Affa me seh Bobo run pon dem dem vex*
Wonder if dem kno wah a come next
Busy lead out di hot head dem
But I man lead out di wrap head dem
Yo Nyahbinghi, Bobo Shanti

Furthermore, Caucasian Bobos like the *tucked-in-shirt-and-turban* Jah Lex from Montreal – who produced a video clip (kingjahlex, 2014) full of Bobo Shanti symbolism and references, including footage from outside of the Bull Bay headquarters and broom-selling Bobos for the programmatic *Bobo Man A Chant* (Jah Lex, 2014) – have been introduced to the scene, reflecting a tendency of internationalization in Jamaican music, as represented by German singer Gentleman or the Jamaica-based Alborosie, who is of Italian origin. On-and-off-Bobos like Ras Shiloh, Cali P., Pressure or Turbulence softened up their militant stance and turned towards a more moderate form of presentation, uncovering their locks and hardly making references to the Order – with few exceptions (Turbulence, 2015). All in all, the *turban people* might have become more rare in videos, on stages, CDs- and magazine-covers, but highly iconic veterans like Sizzla Kalonji (Barnett, 2014) with his socially significant *Judgement Yard* community center in August Town – an area confronted with questions of spacial identity, politics and violence (Charles, 2004) – keep on guarranteeing a rather high visibility compared to other Rastafarian branches.

Conclusion

The aim of this discussion was to shed light on the influence of radical religious thought on popular styles of Black musical expression. Building on existing literature (Miyakawa, 2005; O'Connor, 2006) that is arguing considerable influence of the Five Percent Nation on the opus of commercially relevant Hip Hop artists in the United States, this discussion mainly attempted to evaluate a possible corresponding pattern in the case of the Bobo Shanti Rasta Mansion and Jamaican Dancehall/Reggae. Hence, in order to reach a conclusion, degree, directional patterns and comparability, as well as similarities and differences concerning the articulated doctrine and ideology have been contextualized in the form of a multi-layered, comparative case study.

Five Percenter ideology can clearly be considered as a basic component for the creation and development of Hip Hop culture and Rap music and therefore tends to be more present in the music, during the chosen time segment around the millenial turn, Rap music and Dancehall-Reggae presented themselves as almost equally dominated by proponents of rather obscure, reactionary and radical religious ideas. At least in terms of perceived impact, that is – since the Bobo artists strongly made their presence felt by flashy robes, colorful turbans and demonstrative utterances of *fyah burn*.

As a matter of fact, many of the basic principles inherent to Five Percenter ideology can be attested as being quite compatible with Bobo Shanti doctrine. Strong similarities concerning the directional patterns of both groups' conceptual background – as articulated by affiliated artists – can be detected in basically all of the established categories and summed up by the following paradoxical characteristics:

- ambivalent relation between outspoken Black supremacy and de facto absence of ethnic discrimination

- symbolical shunning of homosexuals, paralleled by community-oriented, social activities and messages

- simultaneously appreciative as well as striking pejorative attitude towards females

- highlighting of moral superiority by frequent references to abstinence from prohibited food and drug consumption on one hand and outspoken glorification of the latter on the other

In more detail, the results in regard to the respective established categories read like this:

A) Re-interpretation of terminology and the establishment of counterknowledge

On the level of lyrical content, Bobo artists proved to stick mainly to the established canon of classical Rastafarian topics – with the exception of the reverence given to King Emmanuel I. Although the re-interpretation of terminology as part of a broader strategy for self-empowerment among Jamaicans, Rastas and Reggae artists has already been acknowledged as a creative form of resistance against colonial forces, Bobo artists developed a slightly enhanced version of this type of *spiritual warfare* that is common among Rastafarian circles. However, the more drastic and aggravated delivery of a seemingly militant rhetoric as well as established symbolical inter-contextualization of Biblical images and contemporary representatives of imperialistic powers – that might partly classify as the construction of counterknowledge – aside, Bobo artists basically abstain from the incorporation of any type of coded system or symbolism. The references present themselves to be very plain, clear and recognizable – from distinguishing looks, to mentionings of the Order's headquarter in Bull Bay or the ever present founding father, King Emmanuel I. Five Percenters on the other hand tend to remain less recognizable in regard to appearance but operate very close to Five Percenter doctrine in the context of lyrical articulation – by quoting or paraphrasing original parts of the group's more or less hidden core lessons.

B) Dogmatic perceptions and symbolism

Given the above mentioned use of coded systems such as the *Supreme Alphabet* or *Supreme Mathematics* among Five Percenters, the delivery of inherent dogmatic principles and corresponding symbolism usually happens on a much more sophisticated level than what is common for Bobo artists. Furthermore, it frequently presents itself to be embedded in a seemingly trivial context that allows for manifold possible meanings and interpretations – fully accessible only to initiated members familiar with the complex esoteric allegories, most probably. Bobo artists on the other hand seem to manifest a reflection of their faith that is much more based on its exoteric appearance by sharing commonplace aspects and duties of worship that allow for rather accessible reception by a broader audience.

C) Attitude towards other religious groups and ethnic discrimination

As demonstrated, both groups make extensive use of reversed racism in a rather radical form. However, while Five Percenters are frequently incorporating their infamous rhetorical claim of *the white man is the devil* into their lyrics, the movement is basically open for non-Black members. As a matter of fact, since everybody who is not a Five Percenter is basically considered as *uncivilized* – including members of all ethnic origin as well as competitive movements such as the Nation of Islam or orthodox Muslims –, although artists usually do not articulate exclusive tendencies towards competitive groups. As a matter of fact, they even tend to occasionally position themselves close to orthodox Islam – which must be labeled as a sort of general absorption of what provided the rough blueprint that their own mythological landscape derived from. In a similar sense, a rather strong rejection of Christianity and its Caucasian depiction of Jesus Christ can be attested that is shared with artists affiliated with the Bobo Shanti. The latter show a tendency to address other followers of the Rastafarian faith for neglecting its religious aspects at times – but are simultaneously criticized by competing branches that label them as rigid extremists.

D) Visibility and declared affiliation of artists

As a matter of fact, although Five Percenters are very widespread in Hip Hop, they tend to be less visible due to the absence of strict formal dress codes and an elaborated system of coded language – that can either be attributed directly to its dogmatic sources or rather be interpreted as a more general statement, stemming from a broad re-contextualization of the ideology in Hip Hop culture. Missing this possible approach of understatement, Bobos display a strong visual presence as a clear minority among Reggae- and Dancehall-artists alike (Judah Asante, 2015).

Nevertheless, the Bobo Shanti tend to look down on Bobo artists as spiritually inferior to those who live a life that is more in accordance to the teachings of their founding father King Emmanuel I in terms of behavior, occupation and the adherence to the Mosaic Law of the Old Testament. Although King Emmanuel I is attributed with giving his personal blessings to artists like Capleton and Junior Reid, the official approach of the Bobo Shanti Order to benefit from the generated popularity was to ease up their restrictions and record their own, non-secular Nyahbinghi songs to participate in the music market. Artists on the other hand are reported to often approach the Order for the sole purpose to obtain permission to use its insignia and vocabulary in their creative output.

E) Moral superiority, dietary approach and attitude towards drugs

Artists affiliated with the Five Percenters would frequently stress their duty as self-styled *righteous teachers* on a mission to *civilize the uncivilized* and therefore demonstrate a rather inclusive approach in addressing those who are still in need of enlightenment. Hence, while intellectual and spiritual advancement is frequently stressed by reference to counterknowledge only accessible to initiates, those who therefore lack a proper understanding in terms of moral conduct and dietary restrictions are not so much condemned for it but rather addressed as victims of a system that keeps them in ignorance. While drug abuse tends to be condemned occasionally, it is found to be glorified as well – which represents the heterogenous position of Five Percenters towards the issue in general. Bobo artists on the contrary clearly shun all involvement in abuse of substances that they would label as drugs in accordance to their doctrine but tend to glorify the use of marijuana outside the context of ceremonial settings – in contrast to the practice of the Order. Practical aspects of their adherence to Bobo Shanti doctrine such as moral standards and abstinence from prohibited alimentation are regularly being articulated from a superior point of view that condemns those that engage in forbidden wordly activities as sinners. Modern lifestyle is often being juxtaposed with *the Ten Commandments* and Old Testamentarian regulations as primary guideline for *righteous* behavior.

F) Attitude towards gender and homosexuality

Artists of both categories clearly tend to reflect the reactionary perspective of their respective ideological background – with conduct and behavior of females expected to be in line with the general setting of the group for them to be considered as honorable. While Five Percenters more frequently depict themselves as misogynists in accordance with the accentuated elements of exaggerated masculinity and braggadocio-attitude in the context of Rap and Hip Hop, Bobo artists often allow for a rather sensitive approach in their performance that seems to be in line with the humbleness expected by adherents to the Rastafarian faith. In both cases, praisal of female virtous mainly revolves around their roles as obedient supporters and mothers. While the use of homophobic statements is happening in a more playful way in the case of Five Percenters – who mainly refer to it in the context of the highly competitive setting characteristic for Rap –, Bobo artists echo a strongly developed shunning of homosexuals that is widespread in Jamaican society and to a considerable degree fueled by religious authorities outside of Rasta circles. However, as compared to Five Percenters – for whom actual homophobia outside their artistic performance does not seem to be an issue –, Bobos tend to take a much less compromising stance and fully refute it despite severe commercial consequences such as bans from radio airplay, concert venues or even countries.

A more aggressive style of delivery aside, the ideological sources of reference for Bobo artists are not much different from those of typical Roots Reggae artists, which makes it difficult to pin down content that can be exclusively attributed to the Order. Clearly distinguishing elements would be limited to certain keywords and phrases like the characteristic *fyah bun*, hints towards the Holy Trinity composed of Haile Selassie I, King Emmanuel I and Marcus Garvey, as well as mentioning of specific dogmatic principles concerning specific aspects of worship or restrictions regarding lifestyle and occupation. In addition, the fact that Bobo Shanti ideology shares more common points with general Rastafarian philosophy than the rather unique Five Percenter doctrine does with the broad spectrum of Islam-inspired movements oriented towards Black Empowerment leads to a seemingly lesser degree of attestable specific influence on Jamaican Dancehall/Reggae – in which Rastafarian-influenced content is but one among many anyway. However, the construction of hybrid identities as perfectionized by artists like Sizzla and Teflon allow to cross clearly defined segments of style and audience more easily.

One of the intended outcomes of this discussion has been to be able to reach towards a possible evaluation of whether the relationship between Bobo artists and the Order can possibly be described as exploitative or symbiotic by defining if artists are using references to the Order to boost their visibility and sales or more likely being used and instrumentalized for spreading radical religious thought to a mass audience. It is obvious that the Order highly benefited from the global popularity and influence of devoted artists such as Sizzla, Capleton or Lutan Fyah without a doubt – enabling them to make their rather conservative and strict presence being felt among more relaxed and open Rasta Mansions and to have their central claims of repatriation, reparation, and the characteristic reverence to King Emmanuel I echoing in the international show business.

At the same time, Bobo artists have been shunned as Taliban for their rigid religious attitude and looked down at by regular Bobo members for their secular occupation. Furthermore, Rastas and Christians alike condemn them for their strong rejection of a white Jesus figure and deem them as anti-Christs or plain racists while on the other hand their religiously justified, homophobic lyrics get them banned from radio stations, concert avenues or even countries. The many secular artists who are facing the same issues are still more successful in commercial terms, so there are not many reasons for Bobo artists to expose themselves from that point of view, except an estimated honest response to their deep convictions and firm beliefs. Any exploitation of the Order's identity for PR purposes or to cross over between markets and segments of the audience would therefore be doomed to backfire at the artist one way or another due to a considerable amount of disadvantages on the long term and therefore seems rather unlikely. If so, it is more the Bobos themselves who borrow from more commercially appealing styles, such as Dancehall, Hip Hop or Rn'B.

Nevertheless, it can be observed that there is a new type of mainstream-oriented artist, that borrows elements of Bobo Shanti-doctrine, -ideology and -appearance and presents a more moderate version of the Order – portraying it as naturally rooted and fully compatible with general Rastafarian philosophy and hence providing the base for a broader establishment of the former radicals. As a possible result, even those who would not explicitly respond to Bobo Shanti doctrine might be able to acknowledge and identify with the ideological legacy of King Emmanuel I – thus freeing him from sectarian associations as well as turning him into a more widely agreed upon integrationist figure. Whether the Bobo elders in Bull Bay like it or not, King Emmanuel I and his *turban people* have become a seal of integrity and authenticity within the Rasta community and – even if not joined in their ranks – at least held in high honor and respect for their strict and uncompromising adherence to the religious core of the faith and its political claims of repatriation in a time where worldwide more and more people are flocking towards Rastafari for fashion purposes. Without their core principles being changed or adjusted, the question remains though, which external factors have rendered the Bobo Shanti from widely shunned radical extremists during the 1990s to casually referrenced regulars in the output of recent Jamaican artists.

However, this work does not claim to be a complete or in-depth account of Bobo Shanti representation in Jamaican popular music but rather used the example of the most relevant, visible and consistent artists affiliated to the Order for a comparative study with similar influence of Five Percenter ideology on US-Hip Hop. More detailed work to measure the impact of the Bobo Shanti Order on the Reggae and Dancehall scene still needs to be done.

References

Ahmed, A. (2012). *Allah and the word: Dissemination of Islamic-based ideologies in Black America* (Doctoral dissertation, Indiana University).

Aidi, H. (2004). "Verily, there is only one hip-hop Umma": Islam, cultural protest and urban marginality. *Socialism and Democracy, 18*(2), 107-126.
doi: 10.1080/08854300408428402

Aidi, H. (2011). The grand (hip-hop) Chessboard: race, rap and raison d'Etat. *Middle East Report, 260*(9/11/11), 25-39.

Aidi, H. (2013). *Rebel Music: Race, Empire, and the New Muslim Youth Culture*. New York: Pantheon.

Akam Entertainment (2013, February 1). Sizzla - Oneness [Peas Inna Pot Riddim] Jan 2013 [Video file]
Retrieved from
https://www.youtube.com/watch?v=O6e0Rkb6tnA

Akam Entertainment (2014, July 8). Educated Dunce [7ven Riddim] July 2014 [Video file]
Retrieved from
https://www.youtube.com/watch?v=CLsAVovZVZ8

Alim, H. S. (2006). Re-inventing Islam with unique modern tones: Muslim hip hop artists as verbal Mujahidin. *Souls, 8*(4), 45-58.

Alim, H. S., Ibrahim, A., & Pennycook, A. (Eds.). (2008). *Global linguistic flows: Hip hop cultures, youth identities, and the politics of language.* London: Routledge.

Anderson, M., & McLean, N. (2014). "Straighten Up Yu Argument": Language as Shibboleth of Jamaican Masculinity. *Caribbean Quarterly, 60*(3), 19-38. doi: 10.1080/00086495.2014.11672524

Atlantic Records (2009, October 26). Brand Nubian Wake Up (Video) [Video file]. Retrieved from https://www.youtube.com/watch?v=TE0J4Ewc1kA

Atteslander, P. (1995). Methoden der empirischen Sozialforschung. Berlin, New York: Walter de Gruyter.

Bailey, J. H. (2006). The final frontier: Secrecy, identity, and the media in the rise and fall of the united nuwaubian nation of moors. *Journal of the American Academy of Religion, 74*(2), 302-323.

Barnett, M. (2002). Rastafari Dialectism: The Epistemological Individualism and Conectivism of Rastafari. *Caribbean Quarterly, 48*(4), 54-61.

Barnett, M. (2005). The many faces of Rasta: Doctrinal Diversity within the Rastafari Movement. *Caribbean Quarterly, 51*(2), 67-78.

Barnett, M. (2006). Differences and Similarities Between the Rastafari Movement and the Nation of Islam. *Journal of Black Studies, 36*(6), 873-893.

Barnett, M. (2014). *Rastafari in the new millennium: A Rastafari reader*. Syracuse, New York: Syracuse University Press.

Bascomb, L. T. (2016). Freakifying history: remixing royalty. *African and Black Diaspora: An International Journal, 9*(1), 57-69.
doi: 10.1080/17528631.2015.1056403

Bax, D. (2010, April 4). "Mich stört diese Doppelmoral". *taz.de*.
Retrieved from
http://www.taz.de/!5144764/

Bayoumi, M. (2001). East of the Sun (West of the Moon): Islam, the Ahmadis, and African America. *Journal of Asian American Studies, 4*(3), 251-263.

Bayoumi, M., & DeCaro, L. (1999). Moorish Science. *Transition*, 80, 100-119.
doi:10.2307/2903171

Bedasse, M. (2010). Rasta Evolution: The Theology of the Twelve Tribes of Israel. *Journal of Black Studies, 40*(5), 960-973.

Bell, D. (2011). *Ode to the downpressor: A psychological portrait of racism, classism, and denial in (post) colonial Jamaica.* Pacifica Graduate Institute.

Bendle, M. F. (2005). The apocalyptic imagination and popular culture. *The Journal of Religion and Popular Culture, 11*(1), 1-1.
doi: 10.3138/jrpc.11.1.001

Berggren, K. (2012). 'No homo': Straight inoculations and the queering of masculinity in Swedish hip hop. *norma, 7*(01), 51-66.

Berkman, F. J. (2007). appropriating Universality: The Coltranes and 1960s spirituality. *American Studies, 48*(1), 41-62.
Retrieved from
https://journals.ku.edu/index.php/amerstud/article/viewFile/3142/3899

Bibi Khan, K. (2012). Erykah Badu and the teachings of the Nation of Gods and Earths. *Muziki, 9*(2), 80-89.
doi: 10.1080/18125980.2012.742237

Blatter, E. (2008). Chant Down Babylon: the Rastafarian Movement and Its Theodicy for the Suffering.
Retrieved from
http://blogs.goucher.edu/verge/files/2016/01/Blatter.pdf

Blauner, R. (1969). Internal colonialism and ghetto revolt. *Social problems, 16*(4), 393-408.

Boboorder (2012, April 5). REGGAY IS DEATH [Video file].
Retrieved from
https://www.youtube.com/watch?v=GHFyLEvIQyk

Bowen, P. D. (2013). *The African-American Islamic Renaissance and the Rise of the Nation of Islam* (Dissertation, Iliff School of Theology).
Retrieved from
http://digitalcommons.du.edu/cgi/viewcontent.cgi?article=1962&context=etd

Boyer, H. C. (1979). Contemporary gospel music. *The Black Perspective in Music, 7*(1), 5-58.

Bracey, B. (2007). *The Journal of African American History, 92*(3), 457-459.

Brown, L. (Ed.). (2010). *John Coltrane and black America's quest for freedom: Spirituality and the music*. Oxford, New York: Oxford University Press.

Brown, J. R. (2011). No homo. *Journal of homosexuality, 58*(3), 299-314.

Burnett, G. W. (2015). *The Gospel According to the Blues*. Cambridge: The Lutterworth Press.

Caponi, G. D. (Ed.). (1999). *Signifyin(g), sanctifyin'& slam dunking: A reader in African American expressive culture*. Amherst: University of Massachusetts Press.

chadwick gillingss (2014, January 7). lutan fyah The only king [Video file]. Retrieved from
https://www.youtube.com/watch?v=MZOHZjB5728

Chaîne de yerpee (2008, June 3). Jah Mason – Mother [Video file]. Retrieved from
https://www.youtube.com/watch?v=HLsHAE9lC3E

Chakravarty, K. G. (2014a). Rastafari Revisited: A Four-Point Orthodox/Secular Typology. *Journal of the American Academy of Religion, 83*(1), 151-180. doi: 10.1093/jaarel/lfu084

Chakravarty, K. G. (2014b). African Nazarites: a comparative religious ethnography of Rastafari and Ibandla lamaNazaretha (Doctoral dissertation, University of Montreal).

Chandler, W. B. (2000). *Ancient Future: The Teachings and Prophetic Wisdom of the Seven Hermetic Laws of Ancient Egypt*. Baltimore: Black Classic Press.

Charles, C. (2004). Political identity and criminal violence in Jamaica: The Garrison community of August Town and the 2002 election. *Social and Economic Studies, 53*(2), 31-73.

Chase, C. W. (2010). Prophetics in the Key of Allah: Towards an Understanding of Islam in Jazz. *Jazz Perspectives, 4*(2), 157-181.

Cheney, C. (1999). Representin'God: Rap, Religion and the Politics of a Culture. *The North Star: A Journal of African American Religious History*, *3*(1), 1-12.
Retrieved from
http://www.princeton.edu/~jweisenf/northstar/volume3/cheney.pdf

Chevannes, B. (1977). The literature of rastafari. *Social and Economic Studies, 26*(1), 239-262.

Chevannes, B. (1990a). Rastafari: Towards a new approach. *Nieuwe West-Indische Gids /New West Indian Guide,64*(3/4), 127-148.

Chevannes, B. (1990b). Healing the Nation: Rastafari exorcism of the ideology of Racism in Jamaica. *Caribbean Quarterly, 36*(1/2), 59-84.

Chevannes, B. (1994). *Rastafari: Roots and ideology.* Syracuse, New York: Syracuse University Press.

Chiu, N. (2005). An Educational Exploration of Homophobia and Sexism in Rap and Hip Hop: Homo-Thugs and Divas in da House. In *FORUM: for promoting 3-19 comprehensive education, 47*(1), 23-29. Symposium Journals.

ChronixxMusic (2011, December 20). Chronixx – Start A Fyah [Video file]. Retrieved from
https://www.youtube.com/watch?v=XF3J9GM_rO0

Clark, L. S. (2006). Introduction to a forum on religion, popular music, and globalization. *Journal for the Scientific Study of Religion, 45*(4), 475-479.

Cooper, C. (2005). *Sweet & Sour Sauce: Sexual Politics in Jamaican Dancehall Culture.* York University/Centre For Research on Latin America and the Caribbean. Retrieved from
http://cerlac.info.yorku.ca/files/2016/08/Cooper.pdf

Constantine-Simms, D. (Ed.). (2001). *The greatest taboo: Homosexuality in Black communities*. Los Angeles: Alyson Publications.

Corbiscello, G. (1998). A Nation of Gods: The Five Percent Nation of Islam. *Journal of Gang Research, 5*(2), 61-73.

Curtis, E. E. (2002). *Islam in Black America: identity, liberation, and difference in African-American Islamic thought*. Albany: SUNY Press.

Curtis, E. E. (2006). *Black Muslim religion in the Nation of Islam, 1960-1975*. Chapel Hill: University of North Carolina Press.

Curtis, E. E., & Sigler, D. B. (Eds.). (2009). *The New Black Gods. Arthur Huff Fausset and the Study of African American Religions*. Bloomington: Indiana University Press.

DancehalDopeBoi (2013, December 7). Aidonia - One Voice [Video file]. Retrieved from
https://www.youtube.com/watch?v=aMOFUYAmpBY

Dancehall Seduction (2014, October 31). Teflon -- Cleanest Bobo |Gud Up Gud Up Riddim| November 2014 [Video file]. Retrieved from https://www.youtube.com/watch?v=x13PRYiPECU

Daniels, M. (2014). The Largest Vocabulary in Hip Hop. Retrieved 2016-08-24 from http://poly-graph.co/vocabulary.html

Davidson, S. (2015). Leave Babylon: The Trope of Babylon in Rastafarian Discourse. *Black Theology. An International Journal, 6*(1), 46-60. doi: 10.1558/blth2008v6i1.46

Davis, A. (2006). Translating Narratives of Masculinity Across Borders: A Jamaican Case Study. *Caribbean Quarterly, 52*(2/3), 22-38.

Decker, J. (1993). The State of Rap: Time and Place in Hip Hop Nationalism. *Social Text, 34,* 53-84. doi:10.2307/466354

deejayedyk (2012, July 27). Yo! MTV Raps-Brand Nubian (1993) [Video file]. Retrieved from https://www.youtube.com/watch?v=Ize0ytRfazo

Dizzy, I. (1967). Ras."The Rastas Speak". *Caribbean Quarterly, 13*(4), 41-42.

djvlad (2013, February 4). Lord Jamar - Lift Up Your Skirt (Kayne West Diss) [Video file].
Retrieved from
https://www.youtube.com/watch?v=v5XvjYcVY6Y

Dorman, J. S. (2016). *Chosen People: The Rise of American Black Israelite Religions*. New York: Oxford University Press.

Edmonds, E. B. (1998). The structure and ethos of Rastafari. In Murrell, N.S. et al. (Eds.). *Chanting Down Babylon. The Rastafari Reader*. Kingston: Ian Randle.

Edmonds, E. B. (2002). *Rastafari: from outcasts to cultural bearers*. Oxford: Oxford University Press.

empress1n3 (2011, September 14). BOBO SHANTI MEMBERS SAY NO TO REGGAE.
Retrieved from
https://www.youtube.com/watch?v=Uywl35arJSM

Essien-Udom, E. U. (1962). *Black nationalism: The search for an identity*. Chicago: University of Chicago Press.

Fairclough, N. (1992). *Discourse and Social Change*. Cambridge: Polity Press.

Fanusie, F. (2007). Ahmadi, Beboppers, Veterans, and Migrants: African American Islam in Boston, 1948–1963. In Trost, T. L. (Ed.). *The African diaspora and the study of religion*. Basingstoke: Palgrave Macmillan.

Finley, S., Guillory, M., & Page Jr., H. (Eds.). (2014). *Esotericism in African American Religious Experience:"there is a Mystery"*... Leiden, Boston: Brill.

Floyd Jr., S. A. (1996). *The power of black music: Interpreting its history from Africa to the United States*. Oxford University Press.

Floyd-Thomas, J. M. (2003). A Jihad of Words: The Evolution of African American Islam and Contemporary Hip-Hop. In: Pinn, A. B. (Ed.). *Noise and spirit: The religious and spiritual sensibilities of rap music*. New York, London: New York University Press.

Full Moon Films (2015, October 9). Prophet Benjamin and Mr. Royal – Just Too Real [Video file].
Retrieved from
https://www.youtube.com/watch?v=S-gyOFhX5Cg

Gansinger, M. (2008). Soziale Artikulation im US-HipHop. Kommunikationsstruktur einer sozialen Minderheit. Saarbrücken: VDM.

Gibbs, M. (2003). ThugGods. Spiritual Darkness and Hip-Hop.
Retrieved from
http://beauty.gmu.edu/HipHop/thuggods.pdf

Girtler, R. (1984). Methoden der qualitativen Sozialforschung. Anleitung zur Feldarbeit. Wien, Köln: Böhlau.

Gold, J. (1989, January 6). Enemy of the People. *LA Weekly*, 14-20.

Goldish, M. (2009). *The Sabbatean Prophets*. Cambridge, London: Harvard University Press.

Gosa, T. L. (2011). Counterknowledge, racial paranoia, and the cultic milieu: Decoding hip hop conspiracy theory. *Poetics*, *39*(3), 187-204.
Retrieved from
http://www.sciencedirect.com/science/article/pii/S0304422X11000167

Gray, B. M. (2014). Show and Prove: Five Percenters and the Study of African American Esotericism. In Finley, S., Guillory, M., & Page Jr., H. *Esotericism in African American Religious Experience:"there is a Mystery"*... Leiden, Boston: Brill.

Gutzmore, C. (2004). Casting the first stone!: Policing of homo/sexuality in Jamaican popular culture. *Interventions*, *6*(1), 118-134.
doi: 10.1080/1369801042000185697

Hamlet, J. D. (1998). Understanding African American oratory: Manifestations of Nommo. In Hamlet, J. D. (Ed.). *Afrocentric visions: Studies in culture and communication*. Thousand Oaks: Sage.

Hannah, B. M. B. (1981). *Rastafari, the New Creation*. Kingston: Jamaica Media Productions.

Harris, F. C. (1999). *Something within: Religion in African-American political activism*. New York: Oxford University Press.

Harrison, F. V. (1988). The politics of social outlawry in urban Jamaica. *Urban Anthropology and Studies of Cultural Systems and World Economic Development, 17*(2/3), 259-277.

Harrison, F. V. (1990). Jamaica and the International Drug Economy. *TransAfrica Forum, 7*(3), 49-58.

Hassell, M. K. (2015). *Under siege: Conspiracy, i-pistemology and resistance through hip hop in Killarmy's Silent Weapons for Quiet Wars* (Doctoral dissertation, The University of Memphis).
Retrieved from
http://search.proquest.com/docview/1728304202

Hill, M. L. (2009). Scared straight: Hip-hop, outing, and the pedagogy of queerness. *The Review of Education, Pedagogy, and Cultural Studies*, *31*(1), 29-54.

Hilliard, A. G. (1985). *Kemetic Concepts of Education: The African Perspective of Education*. London: Hackney Black Peoples Association.

Hilliard, A. G. (1989). Kemetic (Egyptian) historical revision: Implications for cross-cultural evaluation and research in education. *American Journal of Evaluation*, *10*(2), 7-23.

Hope, D. (2006). Dons and shottas: Performing violent masculinity in Dancehall culture. *Social and Economic Studies, 55*(1/2), 115-131.

Hope, D. (2009). 'I Came to Take My Place'. Contemporary Discourses Of Rastafari in Jamaican popular culture. *Revista Brasileira do Caribe, 9*(18), 401-423.

Hope, D. (2012). "Pon di Borderline": Exploring Constructions of Jamaican Masculinity in Dancehall and Roots Theatre. *Journal of West Indian Literature, 21*(1/2), 105-128.

Howell, Joseph T. (1973). *Hard Living on Clay Street: Portraits of Blue Collar Families*. New York: Anchor Books.

Huhtala, M. (2015). The one in the many: expressions of rastafari spirituality (Master's Thesis, University of Tampere).
Retrieved from
https://tampub.uta.fi/bitstream/handle/10024/96930/GRADU-1429516376.pdf?sequence=1

Isma'ilis, N. (2014). Muslim minority groups in American Islam. *The Oxford Handbook of American Islam*. Oxford: Oxford University Press.

Jamaica Explosion Hd (2010, November 1). Lutan Fyah-Length of Days Official Video (HD) [Video file].
Retrieved from
https://www.youtube.com/watch?v=N4KMJq7ulnk

Jauhiainen, M. (2008). Turban and Crown Lost and Regained: Ezekiel 21: 29-32 and Zechariah's Zemah. *Journal of Biblical Literature*, *127*(3), 501-511.

Judah Asante (2015, September 18). Test me if you can 2000 [Video file].
Retrieved from
https://www.youtube.com/watch?v=Hk94J04Phtc

Julien, L. A. (2003). Great Black Warrior Queens: An examination of the gender currents within Rastafari thought and the adoption of a feminist agenda in the Rasta women's movement. *Agenda, 17*(57), 76-84.

doi: 10.1080/10130950.2003.9674478

Kabaka Pyramid (2016, August 11). Kabaka Pyramid – Kabaka vs. Pyramid [Music Video] [Video file].
Retrieved from
https://www.youtube.com/watch?v=PObfY6Ri3BE

Kabbani, M. H. (2003). Classical Islam and the Naqshbandi Sufi Tradition. Fenton: ISCA.

Kamimoto, S. (2015). Influence of Reggae Music on the Economic Activities of EABIC Rastafarians in Jamaica. *Caribbean Quarterly, 61*(1), 42-59.
doi:10.1080/00086495.2015.11672547

Karenga M., & Carruthers J. (Eds.). (1986). Kemet and the African worldview. Los Angeles: University of Sankore Press.

Kelley, R. D. (2012). *Africa speaks, America answers: Modern jazz in revolutionary times*. Cambridge, London: Harvard University Press.

Khabeer, S. A. (2007). Rep that Islam1: the rhyme and reason of American Islamic hip hop. *The Muslim World, 97*(1), 125-141.

Khan, K. B. (2012). Signifying the monkey: rhetorical modes of expressions in African American music: the case of KRS-One. *Muziki, 9*(1), 35-57. doi:10.1080/18125980.2012.737103

Killmann, P. (2014). Unter Göttern – 50 Jahre Five Percent Nation. *All Good*. Retrieved from http://allgood.de/features/reportagen/unter-goettern-50-jahre-five-percent-nation/

kingjahlex (2014, July 27). Capleton, Jah Lex & Selaska. 'Bobo Man a Chant' Official Video [Video file].
Retrieved from https://www.youtube.com/watch?v=W29QUcPw3Fg

Kister, M. J. (2000). "The Crowns of This Community"...: Some Notes on the Turban in the Muslim Tradition. *Jerusalem Studies in Arabic and Islam, 24*(1), 217-245.

Kitzinger, S. (1969). Protest and Mysticisim: The Rastafari Cult of Jamaica. *Journal for the Scientific Study of Religion, 8*(2), 240-262.

Knight, M. M. (2013). *The five percenters: Islam, hip-hop and the Gods of New York*. Oxford: Oneworld Publications.

Kornegay Jr, E. L. (2013). Between James's Gospel and Jimmy's blues. In Kornegay Jr, E. L. (Ed.). *A Queering of Black Theology*. Basingstoke: Palgrave Macmillan.

Krish Genius Music (2014, October 8). Bugle - Survivor [7th Heaven Riddim] October 2014 [Video file].
Retrieved from
https://www.youtube.com/watch?v=W3VvjhV145o

Krish Genius Music (2015, December 4). Rasta Party [Official Music Video] [Video file]. Retrieved from
https://www.youtube.com/watch?v=XWHiRMK4kr0

Krish Genius Music (2016, May 7). Sizzla - Greatest Mother [Official Music Video] [Video file].
Retrieved from
https://www.youtube.com/watch?v=bMK8Cbi05QQ

KRS ONE (2009). The Gospel of Hip Hop. New York: Powerhouse.

LaFont, S. (2009). Not Quite Redemption Song. In Murray, D. A. B. (Ed.). *Homophobias: Lust and Loathing across Time and Space*. Durkham and London: Duke University Press.

Larcher, A. A., & Robinson, C. (2009). Fighting Murder Music: Activist Reflections. *Caribbean Journal of Gender Studies, 3,* 1-12.
Retrieved from
https://sta.uwi.edu/crgs/november2009/journals/akimadelarcher.pdf

Leach, E. (1966). Ritualization in Man in Relation to Conceptual and Social Development. *Philosophical Transactions of the Royal Society of London. Series B, Biological Sciences, 251*(772). A Discussion on Ritualization of Behaviour in Animals and Man (Dec. 29, 1966), pp. 403-408.

Lincoln, C. E. (1974). *The black experience in religion*. New York: Anchor Books.

Lovell, J. (1972). *Black Song: The Forge and the Flame: The Story of How the Afro-American Spiritual Was Hammered Out*. St. Paul: Paragon House Publishers.

Mack, D. R. (1999). *From Babylon to Rastafari: Origin and history of the Rastafarian movement*. Chicago: Frontline Distribution International.

Marshall, W. (2006). Bling-Bling for Rastafari: How Jamaicans deal with Hip-Hop. *Social and Economic Studies, 55*(1/2), 49-74.

Maultsby, P. K. (2000). *Afrikanisms in African-American Music. A turbulent voyage: Readings in African American Studies* (3rd Edition). Lanham: Rowman and Littlefield.

McCloud, A. B. (2014). *African American Islam*. London, New York: Routledge.

McGlashen, G. (2013). Badman or Badman-tu: Defining Badman artiste through popular cultural forms reggae and dancehall.
Retrieved from
http://www.inter-disciplinary.net/criticalissues/wpcontent/uploads/2013/04/McGlashen-up3_dpaper.pdf

McMurray, A. (2007). Hotep and Hip-Hop: Can Black Muslim Women Be Doum with Hip-Hop? *Meridians, 8*(1), 74-92.

Means Coleman, R. R., & Cobb, J. (2007). No way of seeing: Mainstreaming and selling the gaze of homo-thug hip-hop. *Popular Communication, 5*(2), 89-108.

Miah, S., & Kalra, V. S. (2008). Muslim hip-hop: Politicisation of kool Islam. *South Asian Cultural Studies Journal, 2*(1), 12-25.

Miller, M. A. (1993). The Rastafarian in Jamaican Political Culture: The Marginalization of a Change Agent. *The Western Journal of Black Studies, 17*(2), 112-177.

Miller, M. R., Pinn, A. B., & Freeman, B. (Eds.). (2015). *Religion in hip hop: Mapping the new terrain in the US*. London: Bloomsbury Publishing.

Mitchell, T. (2001). *Global noise: Rap and hip hop outside the USA*. Middletown: Wesleyan University Press.

Mitchell-Kernan, C. (1999). Signifying, loud-talking and marking. In Caponi, G. D. (Ed.). *Signifyin(g), sanctifyin'& slam dunking: A reader in African American expressive culture*. Amherst: University of Massachusetts Press.

Miyakawa, F. M. (2005). *Five Percenter rap: God hop's music, message, and black Muslim mission*. Bloomington: Indiana University Press.

Monson, I. (2000). Art Blakey's African Diaspora. In Monson, I. (Ed.). *The African Diaspora: A Musical Perspective*. London, New York: Routledge.

Murder inna Dancehall – 'Nuff with da Chi Chi Man songs! (n. d.). Retrieved from http://www.soulrebels.org/dancehall/e_songs_more.htm

Murray, D. A. B. (2009). *Homophobias: Lust and Loathing across Time and Space*. Durkham, London: Duke University Press.

Murrell, N. S. (2000). Tuning Hebrew Psalms to Reggae Rhythms: Rastas' Revolutionary Lamentations for Social Change. *CrossCurrents, 50*(4), 525-540.

Murrell, N. S., Spencer, W. D. & McFarlane, A. A. (Eds.). (1998). *Chanting Down Babylon. The Rastafari Reader.* Kingston: Ian Randle.

Niiah, J. (2005). Sensitive Scholarship: A Review of Rastafari Literature(s). *Caribbean Quarterly, 51*(3/4), 11-34.

Niiah, J. (2011). Nettleford and Rastafari's Inner Landscape. *Caribbean Quarterly, 57*(3/4), 49-63.

Nobles, W. W. (1986). Ancient Egyptian thought and the renaissance of African (Black) psychology. In Karenga, M., & Carruthers, J. (Eds.). *Kemet and the African worldview.* Los Angeles: University of Sankore Press.

Nuruddin, Y. (2006). Ancient black astronauts and extraterrestrial jihads: Islamic science fiction as urban mythology. *Socialism and Democracy, 20*(3), 127-165.

Olivier, L. (2010). Greeting rituals as everyday management of differences among RasTafari groups in Stellenbosch. *Anthropology Southern Africa, 33*(3/4), 126-131.

Owens, J. V. (1977). Literature on the Rastafari: 1955-1974. *Journal of Ethnic and Migration Studies, 6*(1-2), 150-164.

O'Connor, K. M. (1998). The Islamic Jesus: Messiahhood and Human Divinity in African American Muslim Exegesis. *Journal of the American Academy of Religion, 66*(3), 493-532.

O'Connor, K. M. (2006). Alternative to 'Religion' in an African American Islamic Community: The Five Percent Nation of Gods and Earths. *Introduction to New and Alternative Religions in America, 5*, 23-58.

Palmer, S. J. (2010). *The Nuwaubian Nation: Black Spirituality and State Control.* Farnham: Ashgate Publishing.

Pereira, J. (1998). Babylon to Vatican: Religion in the Dance Hall. *Journal of West Indian Literature, 8*(1), 31-40.

Pinn, A. B. (Ed.). (2003). *Noise and spirit: The religious and spiritual sensibilities of rap music.* New York, London: New York University Press.

Pinn, A. B. (2007). Bling and Blessings: Thoughts on the intersections of Rap music and religious meaning. *CrossCurrents, 57*(2), 289-295.

Pollard, V. (1982). The social history of Dread Talk. *Caribbean Quarterly, 28*(4), 17-40.

Pologod (2014, April 11). SourceTV Exclusive: Tenured Five Percenter sheds light on the Jay-Z controversy. *The Source.*

Retrieved from

http://thesource.com/2014/04/11/thesource-com-exclusive-tenured-five-percenter-sheds-light-on-the-jay-z-controversy/

Poutiainen, A., & Rantakallio, I. (2016). Discursive Construction of African-American Identities and Spirituality: A Comparison of Muslim Hip Hop and 1960s Jazz Avant-Garde. *Popular Music and Society, 39*(2), 186-201.

doi: 10.1080/03007766.2015.1048063

Price, C. R. (2003). Social change and the development and co-optation of a black antisystemic identity: The case of Rastafarians in Jamaica. *Identity: An International Journal of Theory and Research, 3*(1), 9-27.

Rachell, L. E. (2007, January). Cracking the Kemetic code. In *NAAAS Conference Proceedings* (p. 1114). National Association of African American Studies.

rasorder (2009, June 5). CAPLETON & SIZZLA CONTROVERSY 1998 [Video file]. Retrieved from

https://www.youtube.com/watch?v=SvbHMpnzAUM

Rausch, A. J. (2011). *I am hip-hop: conversations on the music and culture.* Lanham: Scarecrow Press.

Realest Entertainment (2014, May 11). Sizzla - Mama Pain - May 2014 [Video file]. Retrieved from https://www.youtube.com/watch?v=9_Pbn0HA2XI

Reed, T. L. (2003). *The holy profane: Religion in black popular music*. Lexington: University Press of Kentucky.

Roberts, Tanaka (2011). Lutan Fyah in the defence of Reggae music. *Jamaicansmusic.com*. Retrieved from http://www.jamaicansmusic.com/news/Interviews/Lutan_Fyah_In_The_Defence_Of_Reggae_Music

Rommen, T. (2006). Protestant Vibrations? Reggae, Rastafari, and Conscious Evangelicals. *Popular Music, 25*(2), 235-263.

Rowe, M. (1980). The woman in Rastafari. *Caribbean Quarterly, 26*(4), 13-21.

Rubenstein, H., & Suarez, C. (1994). The Twelve Tribes of Israel: An Explorative Field Study. *Religion Today, 9*(2), 1-6.

RZA (2009). *The Tao of Wu*. New York: Riverhead Books.

Sanneh, K., & Priest, K. (1997). The Secret Doctrine. *Transition,74*, 162-182.

doi: 10.2307/2935378

Şarlak, E., Onurel, R., Koleksiyon, B., & Kayıt, G. (2014). Depictions Of Prophet Solomon In Christian Icons And Ottoman Miniature Art. *Mediterranean Archaeology and Archaeometry, 14*(1), 321-345.

Savishinsky, N. J. (1994a). Transnational popular culture and the global spread of the Jamaican Rastafarian movement. *NWIG: New West Indian Guide / Nieuwe West-Indische Gids, 68*(3/4), 259-281.

Savishinsky, N. J. (1994b). The Baye Faal of Senegambia: Muslim rastas in the promised land? *Africa-London-International African Institute, 64*(2), 211-219.

doi: 10.2307/1160980

Schaefer, N. A. (2004). Y2K as an Endtime Sign: Apocalypticism in America at the fin-de-millennium. *The Journal of Popular Culture, 38*(1), 82-105.

Semaj, L. (2013). From Peace and Love to 'Fyah Bun': Did Rastafari Lose Its Way?. *Caribbean Quarterly, 59*(2), 96-108.

doi: 10.1080/00086495.2013.11672485

Shimeles, N. (2010). I Love My Niggas No Homo. Homophobia and the Capitalist Subversion of Violent Masculinity in Hip-Hop. *CTSJ: Journal of Undergraduate Research*, *1*(1), 11-37.
Retrieved from
http://scholar.oxy.edu/cgi/viewcontent.cgi?article=1018&context=ctsj

Simons, H. (Ed.). (1980). *Towards a science of the singular: Essays about case study in educational research and evaluation*. Norwich: University of East Anglia, Centre for Applied Research in Education.

Simpson, G. E. (1955). The Ras Tafari movement in Jamaica: A study of race and class conflict. *Social Forces*, *34*(2), 167-171.

Simpson, G. E. (1985). Religion and Justice: Some Reflections on the Rastafari Movement. *Phylon (1960-)*, *46*(4), 286-291.
doi:10.2307/274868

Singh, S. (2004). Resistance, Essentialism, and Empowerment in Black Nationalist Discourse in the African Diaspora: A Comparison of the Back to Africa, Black Power, and Rastafari Movements. *Journal of African American Studies*, *8*(3), 18-36.

Slade, B. (2013). Overstanding Idren: Special Features of Rastafari English Morphology. In *Proceedings of the 2nd Rastafari Studies Conference & General Assembly* (pp. 12-16).

Smith, D. A. (2007). Droppin' Science Fiction: Signification and Singularity in the Metapocalypse of Du Bois, Baraka, and Bell. *Science Fiction Studies, 34*(2), 201-219.

Smith, R. (1998). Black Religious Nationalism and the Politics of Transcendence. *Journal of the American Academy of Religion,66*(3), 533-547.

Smith, M. G., Augier, R., & Nettleford, R. (1967). The Rastafari Movement In Kingston, Jamaica. PART 1. *Caribbean Quarterly, 13*(3), 3-29.

Smitherman, G. (1997). "The Chain Remain the Same". Communicative Practices in the Hip Hop Nation. *Journal of Black Studies, 28*(1), 3-25.

Soares, B. F. (2010). "Rasta" Sufis and Muslim youth culture in Mali. *Being young and Muslim: New cultural politics in the global south and north*, 241-57.

Sorett, J. (2009). 'Believe me, this pimp game is very religious': Toward a religious history of hip hop. *Culture and Religion, 10*(1), 11-22. doi:10.1080/14755610902786288

Spencer, J. M. (1991). *Protest & praise: Sacred music of black religion.* Minneapolis: Fortress Press.

Spencer, J. M. (1995). *The rhythms of Black folk: race, religion, and pan-Africanism.* New Jersey: Africa World Press.

Soumahoro, M. (2007). Christianity on Trial: The Nation of Islam and the Rastafari, 1930-1950. In Trost, T. L. (Ed.). *The African diaspora and the study of religion.* Basingstoke: Palgrave Macmillan.

Spiteri, S. (2014). Female sex tourism in Jamaica: An arena for adaptation and recreation for marginalized men (Master's Thesis, McMaster University, Ontario).

Stake, R. E. (1995). *The art of case study research.* Thousand Oaks: Sage.

Stanley, S. (2005). 'Dis Slackness Ting': A Dichotomizing Master Narrative in Jamaican Dancehall. *Caribbean Quarterly, 51*(3/4), 55-76.

Stjernholm, S. (2011). *Lovers of Muhammad: A Study of Naqshbandi-Haqqani Sufis in the Twenty-First Century* (Doctoral dissertation, Lund University).
Retrieved from
http://lup.lub.lu.se/record/1939383

Stowe, D. W. (2010). Both American and Global: Jazz and World Religions in the United States. *Religion Compass, 4*(5), 312-323.

Sullivan, J. (2007). Understanding and overstanding: religious reading in historical perspective. *Journal of Education and Christian Belief, 11*(2), 25-38.

Swedenburg, T. (1996, November). Islam in the mix: Lessons of the five percent. In *Proceedings from American Anthropological Association Annual Meetings.* Retrieved from

http://www.ucs.mun.ca/~jporter/Swedenborg_5-Percent-Islam.pdf

Swedenburg, T. (2001). Islamic Hip-Hop vs. Islamophobia: Aki Nawaz, Natacha Atlas, Akhenaton. In Mitchell, T. (Ed.). *Global noise: Rap and hip hop outside the USA.* Middletown: Wesleyan University Press.

Swedenburg, T. (2002). Snipers and the Panic Over Five Percent Islamic Hip-Hop. *Middle East Research and Information Project.*
Retrieved from
http://www.merip.org/mero/mero111002

Tafari, I. J. (1995). *A Rastafari View of Marcus Mosiah Garvey.* Kingston: Great Company JA Ltd..

Taiyuan (2008, September 12). Sizzla – Remember [Video file].
Retrieved from
https://www.youtube.com/watch?v=fj5a63TuxUU

Tanis, J. (2010). Babylon by Tro-Tro: The Varieties of Rasta Identity and Practice in Ghana.

Retrieved from

http://digitalcollections.sit.edu/cgi/viewcontent.cgi?article=1844&context=isp_collection

Taylor, M. A. (2005). The Evolutionary Basis and Function of Religion. University of Tennessee Honors Thesis Projects.

Retrieved 2016-10-30 from

http://trace.tennessee.edu/utk_chanhonoproj/921

Threatrics The 3rd (2013, February 9). Brand Nubian Allah U Akbar (Official HD Video) [Video file].

Retrieved from

https://www.youtube.com/watch?v=9mX--czAFqw

Till, R. (2010). *Pop cult: religion and popular music*. London: A&C Black.

Tinaz, N. (1996). The Nation of Islam: historical evolution and transformation of the movement. *Journal of Muslim Minority Affairs*, *16*(2), 193-209.

doi: 10.1080/13602009608716338

Tinaz, N. (2000). Global Impacts of an Ethno-religious Movement: The case of Nation of Islam (NOI) in Britain. *Journal of Economic and Social Research*, *4*(2), 45-71.

Tinaz, N. (2001). *Conversion of African Americans to Islam: a sociological analysis of the Nation of Islam and associated groups* (Doctoral dissertation, University of Warwick).

Trost, T. L. (Ed.). (2007). *The African diaspora and the study of religion*. Basingstoke: Palgrave Macmillan.

Turner, R. B. (2003). *Moorish Science: Islam in the African-American Experience* (2nd Edition). Bloomington: Indiana University Press.

Turner, T. E. (1991). Women, Rastafari and the New Society: Caribbean and East African roots of a popular movement against structural adjustment. *Labour, Capital and Society / Travail, Capital Et Société, 24*(1), 66-89.

Tutturen Nilsson, K. (2013). Social work within a Jamaican Rastafarian community-A study of values regarding women.
Retrieved from
https://lup.lub.lu.se/student-papers/search/publication/3349530

Universal Shaamgaud Allah (n. d.). The Universal Flag by Universal Shaamgaud Allah. *The 5% Nation of the Gods and Earths in Love Allah*. Retrieved 2016-10-31 from http://ngeinla.weebly.com/the-universal-flag-by-universal-shaamgaud-allah.html

unpluggedmm (2015, April 26). Bugle False Prophet official music video [Video file]. Retrieved from
https://www.youtube.com/watch?v=R37EoWWy__M

Van Dijk, F. (1995). Sociological means: Colonial reactions to the radicalization of Rastafari in Jamaica, 1956-1959. *NWIG: New West Indian Guide / Nieuwe West-Indische Gids, 69*(1/2), 67-101.
Retrieved from
http://www.jstor.org/stable/41849658

VISAO3 (2009, December 15). JUNIOR REID – FUNNY MAN [Video file].
Retrieved from
https://www.youtube.com/watch?v=_tzPoRK84PQ

Wahab, A. (2016). Calling 'Homophobia' into Place (Jamaica). *Interventions, 18*(6), 908-928.
doi: 10.1080/1369801X.2015.1130641

Walker, K. (2005). *Dubwise: Reasoning from the reggae underground.* Toronto, Ontario: Insomniac Press.

Walker, F. R., & Kuykendall, V. (2005). Manifestations of nommo in Def Poetry. *Journal of Black Studies, 36*(2), 229-247.

Warner-Lewis, M. (1993). African continuities in the Rastafari belief system. *Caribbean Quarterly, 39*(3/4), 108-123.

Washington, T. N. (2014). Rapping with the Gods: Hip Hop as a Force of Divinity and Continuity from the Continent to the Cosmos. *Journal of Pan African Studies, 6*(9), 72-101.

Waters, A. M. (1985). *Race, class, and political symbols: Rastafari and reggae in Jamaican politics*. Brunswick: Transaction Publishers.

Werner, C. H. (2006). *A change is gonna come: music, race & the soul of America*. Ann Arbor: University of Michigan Press.

Wexler, P. L. (1994). Rastafarian Spirit Replacing Violence in Dancehall Lyrics. *Billboard, 106*(47), 1-2.

"What happened to One Love? Prejudice and Homophobic Violence in Jamaica" (2004, Fall). *OUTfront – For Lesbian, Gay, Bisexual and Transgender Human Rights*. Retrieved from
http://www.amnestyusa.org/pdfs/Newsletter2004.pdf

White, C. (2007). Living in Zion: Rastafarian Repatriates in Ghana, West Africa. *Journal of Black Studies, 37*(5), 677-709.

White, C. M. (2012). Rastafarian repatriates and the negotiation of place in Ghana. *Ethnology: An International Journal of Cultural and Social Anthropology, 49*(4), 303-320.

Williams-Jones, P. (1975). Afro-American gospel music: a crystallization of the black aesthetic. *Ethnomusicology, 19*, 373-385.

Wilson, O. (1974). The significance of the relationship between Afro-American music and West African music. *The Black Perspective in Music, 2*, 3-22.

Wilson, D. (2007). Post-Pomo Hip-Hop Homos: Hip-Hop Art, Gay Rappers, and Social Change. *Social Justice, 34*(1), 117-140.

Witvliet, T. (1985). A Place in the Sun. *An Introduction to Liberation Theology in the Third World.* New York: Maryknoll.

Witvliet, T. (1987). In Search of a Black Christology: The Dialectic of Cross and Resurrection. *CrossCurrents, 37*(1), 17-32.

www.black-king.net
Ethiopian African Black International Congress
Retrieved from
http://www.black-king.net/e.a.b.i.c.%20constitution.htm

Yancy, G. (2004). Geneva Smitherman: The social ontology of African-American language, the power of Nommo, and the dynamics of resistance and identity through language. *The Journal of Speculative Philosophy, 18*(4), 273-299.

Yin, R. K. (1984). Case study research: Design and methods. Newbury Park: Sage.

Zips, W. (2000, November). Die Stadt auf dem Hügel. Der radikale Rasta-Orden Bobo Shanti öffnet sich dem Showgeschäft. *Die Wochenzeitung, 47*(23), 4-5.

Zips, W. & Kämpfer, H. (2001). *Nation X. Schwarzer Nationalismus, Black Exodus und Hip Hop*. Wien: Promedia.

Zips, W. (2003). Pure Militancy. Bobo Ashanti – Radikale Rastafari Propheten im Dancehall Reggae. In Rossbach de Olmos, L., & Schmidt, B. (Eds.). *Ideen über Afroamerika–Afroamerikaner und ihre Ideen: Beiträge der Regionalgruppe Afroamerika auf der Tagung der Deutschen Gesellschaft für Völkerkunde in Göttingen 2001*. Marburg: Curupira.

Zips, W. (2005). Bobo Shanti – Divine Salvation. *Riddim. Reggae, Dancehall, Tunes, Culture*, 2, 56-61.

Zips, W. (2006). (Ed.). *Rastafari: A Universal Philosophy in the Third Millenium*. Kingston: Ian Randle

Zips, W. (2011). There ain't just Black in the Atlantic, Jack! Transformations of Masculinity from the Outlaw to the Rebel in Dancehall Reggae. *Volume!*, *8*(2), 124-159.

Zips, W. (2015). *Hail di Riddim. Reportagen aus dem Reggaeversum*. Wien: Promedia.

Zulu, I. M. (2006). Axioms of Kemet: Instructions for Today from Ancient Egypt. *The Journal of Pan African Studies (Online)*, *1*(6), 1.

Discography

Anthony B. (1996). Fire Pon Rome. On *Real Revolutionary* [CD]. London: Greensleeves.

Beenie Man (1999). Protect Me. On *The Doctor* [CD]. New York: VP.

Beenie Man (2001). Selassie. On *Youth Quake* [CD]. New York: Artists only!.

Brand Nubian (1990a). Wake Up. On *One For All* [LP]. New York: Elektra.

Brand Nubian (1990b). Drop The Bomb. On *One For All* [LP]. New York: Elektra.

Brand Nubian (1990c). *One For All* [LP]. New York: Elektra.

Brand Nubian (1990d). Dance To My Ministry. On *One For All* [LP]. New York: Elektra.

Brand Nubian (1992). Punks Jump Up To Get Beat Down [12-inch Single]. New York: Elektra.

Brand Nubian (1993a). Ain't No Mystery. On *In God We Trust*. [LP]. New York: Elektra.

Brand Nubian (1993b). Allah U Akbar. On *In God We Trust*. [LP]. New York: Elektra.

Brand Nubian (1993c). Allah & Justice. On *In God We Trust*. [LP]. New York: Elektra.

Brand Nubian (1993d). Love Me Or Leave Me Alone. On *In God We Trust*. [LP]. New York: Elektra.

Brand Nubian (1993e). Black Star Line. On *In God We Trust*. [LP]. New York: Elektra.

Brand Nubian (1998a). U For Me. On *Foundation* [LP]. New York: Arista.

Brand Nubian (1998b). Sincerely. On *Foundation* [LP]. New York: Arista.

Bugle (2015). Rope. On *Tough Times Riddim* [Digital]. Hungry Lion Records.

Buju Banton (1992). Boom Bye Bye. [7-inch Single]. New York: VP.

Buju Banton (1995). Murderer. On *'Til Shiloh* [CD]. London: Island.

Capleton (1995). Wings Of The Morning. On *Prophecy* [LP]. New York: Def Jam.

Capleton (2000). Bun Dung Dreddie. On *More Fire* [CD]. New York: VP.

Capleton (2001). Bun Out Di Chi Chi. [7-inch Single]. Kingston: Footsteps.

Capleton (2002). Pure Woman. On *Still Blazin* [LP]. New York: VP.

Capleton (2003). Bun Dem Every Day. [7-inch Single]. Leipzig: Germaican.

Capleton (2004). Fire Haffi Burn. On *Reign of Fire* [LP]. New York: VP.

Culture (1977). Two Sevens Clash. On *Two Sevens Clash* [LP]. Kingston: Joe Gibbs.

Decipher73i (2011). *I Of The Heavens*. [CD]. Insane Asylum Multimedia.

Gangstarr (1992). Conspiracy. On *Daily Operation* [LP]. New York: Chrysalis/EMI.

Gangstarr (1999). Above The Clouds. On *Moment Of Truth* [LP]. New York: Virgin.

Ghostface Killah (1996a). Wildflower. On *Ironman* [LP]. New York: Epic.

Ghostface Killah (1996b). All That I Got Is You. On *Ironman* [LP]. New York: Epic.

Ghostface Killah (1996c). *Ironman* [LP]. New York: Epic.

GZA (2008). Alphabets. On *Pro Tools* [LP]. New York: Babygrande.

Hasan Salaam (2004). Jummah. On *Mixtape Vol. 2* [Digital]. New York: 5th COLUMN Media.

Hasan Salaam (2005a). Tales Of The Lost Tribe. On *Tales Of The Lost Tribe: Hidden Jewels* [CD]. New York: 5th COLUMN Media.

Hasan Salaam. (2005b). Prayer Of A Sinner. On *Paradise Lost* [CD]. New York: Day by Day Entertainment.

Hasan Salaam (2008a). Kingdom Of Heaven. On *Children Of God* [CD]. New York: Truth Medicine Media.

Inspectah Deck (1999). Show And Prove. On *Uncontrolled Substance* [LP]. New York: Loud.

Jah Lex (2014). Bobo Man A Chant. On *Shine Yuh Light* [CD]. Montreal: Alexandre Corbeil.

Jah Mason (2010). Mama. On *Keep Ya Head Up* [CD]. Fort Lauderdale: Rastar.

Jedi Mind Tricks (1996). *The Amber Probe E.P.* [12-inch Single]. Superregular Recordings.

J-Live (1998). The Best Part. On *The Best Part* [LP]. New York: Triple Threat.

Junior Reid (2000). *Emmanuel Calling* [CD]. Kingston: JR Productions.

Junior Reid (2002a). Hat Over Turban. On *Rasta Government* [CD]. Kingston: JR Productions.

Junior Reid (2002b). Man A Nuh Taliban. On *Rasta Government* [CD]. Kingston: JR Productions.

Junior Reid (2007). Love Mama. On *Why I'm Hot* (Official Mixtape CD).

Kabaka Pyramid (2013a). Worldwide Love. On *Lead The Way* [CD]. Kingston: Bebble Rock Records.

Kabaka Pyramid (2013b). Warrior. On *Lead The Way* [CD]. Kingston: Bebble Rock Records.

Kabaka Pyramid (2013c). Lead The Way. On *Lead The Way* [CD]. Kingston: Bebble Rock Records.

Kabaka Pyramid (2013d). Liberal Opposer. On *Lead The Way* [CD]. Kingston: Bebble Rock Records.

King Ital Rebel (2016a). Jah Warrior. On *Rebel Chant* [CD]. Kingston, New York: Jamrockvybz.

King Ital Rebel (2016b). Show Love. On *Rebel Chant* [CD]. Kingston, New York: Jamrockvybz.

Lord Jamar (2006a). Supreme Mathematics. On *The 5% Album*. [CD]. New York: Babygrande.

Lord Jamar (2006b). *The 5% Album*. [CD]. New York: Babygrande.

Lord Jamar (2006c). I.S.L.A.M. On *The 5% Album*. [CD]. New York: Babygrande.

Lord Jamar (2006d). Deep Space. On *The 5% Album*. [CD]. New York: Babygrande.

Lord Jamar (2006e). Original Man. On *The 5% Album*. [CD]. New York: Babygrande.

Lutan Fyah (2004). Ghetto Stress. On *Dem No Know Demselves*. [CD]. Hamburg: Minor 7 Flat 5.

Lutan Fyah (2008a). Word, Sound And Power. On *African Be Proud* [CD]. Kingston: Rastar.

Lutan Fyah (2008b). Watch Over Me. On *Africa* [2CD]. San Francisco: 2B1.

Lutan Fyah (2008c). Rasta Set The Trend. On *Africa* [2CD]. San Francisco: 2B1.

Lutan Fyah (2011a). Genesis. On *The E.P* [EP]. Culture Town.

Lutan Fyah (2011b). Trials And Crosses. On *Sweet Corn Riddim* [Digital]. Pure Music Productions.

Lutan Fyah (2011c). Break I Down. On *Alive Riddim* [Digital]. Dynasty Records.

Lutan Fyah (2011d). Mama Don't Cry. On *Raw Moon Riddim* [Digital]. Master Kat Productions.

Lutan Fyah (2012). Don't Mek Mama Bawl. On *Official Mixtape 2012*. Retrieved from
https://lutanfyah.wordpress.com/

Lutan Fyah (2013). Nuh Cross Mi Line. On *Jamrock Riddim* [Digital]. 12 To 12 Music.

Lutan Fyah (2014). Mama Love. On *Four Seasons Riddim* [Digital]. Union World Music.

Lutan Fyah (2015a). Intro. On *More Blessings* [EP]. Pay Day Music.

Lutan Fyah (2015b). Cyaah Gwaan To Rhatid. On *More Blessings* [EP]. Pay Day Music.

Masta Buildas (2009). *Reptilian Body Snatchas* [CD]. Philadelphia: Nod Records.

Midnite (2001). Enough For Everyone. On *Nemozian Rasta* [CD]. St. Croix: I Grade.

Poor Righteous Teachers (1996a).Word Iz Life. On *The New World Order* [LP]. New York: Profile.

Poor Righteous Teachers (1996b). Gods, Earths and 85ers. On *The New World Order* [LP]. New York: Profile.

Pressure (2011). It Haffi Guh Suh. *Jah Army Riddim* [Digital]. Ghetto Youth International.

Proteje (2013). I&I. On *The 8 Year Affair* [CD]. Kingston: Don Corleon Records.

Rakim (1997). Mystery (Who Is God?). On *The 18th Letter* [LP]. New York: Universal.

Sizzla (1995). No White God. [7-inch Single]. Kingston: Xterminator.

Sizzla (1997a). King In This Jungle. [7-inch Single]. Kingston: Harmony House.

Sizzla (1997b). No Other Like Jah. On *Praise Yeh Jah* [LP]. Kingston: Xterminator.

Sizzla (1997c). Kings Of The Earth [7-inch Single]. Kingston: Xterminator.

Sizzla (1997d). One Away. On *Black Woman And Child* [CD]. New York: VP.

Sizzla (1997e). Give Dem Ah Ride. On *Black Woman And Child* [CD]. New York: VP.

Sizzla (1997f). Black Woman And Child. On *Black Woman And Child* [CD]. New York: VP.

Sizzla (1997g). Praise Yeh Jah On *Praise Yeh Jah* [LP]. Kingston: Xterminator.

Sizzla (1998a). Pure & Clean. On *Hotter Than Fire* [CD]. Kingston: Genesis.

Sizzla (1998b). Clean Up Your Heart. [7-inch Single]. Kingston: X-rated.

Sizzla (1998c). Protect Us and Bless Us. On *Good Ways* [CD]. New York: VP.

Sizzla (1998d). Lovely Morning. On *Kalonji* [CD]. Kingston: Xterminator.

Sizzla (1998e). Good Ways. On *Good Ways* [CD]. New York: VP.

Sizzla (1998f). Aznaldo. On *Good Ways* [CD]. New York: VP.

Sizzla (2000a). *Bobo Ashanti* [CD]. London: Greensleeves.

Sizzla (2000b). Words of Truth. On *Words Of Truth* [CD]. New York: VP.

Sizzla (2000c). Lift Mine Eyes. On *Words Of Truth* [CD]. New York: VP.

Sizzla (2001). Pump Up [7-inch Single]. Kingston: Black Shadow.

Sizzla (2002a). Words, Power And Sound. On *Hosanna* [CD]. Charlotte: Reggae Central.

Sizzla (2002b). Like Mountains. [7-inch Single]. Kingston: Firehouse Crew.

Sizzla (2002c). Mash Dem Down. On *Da Real Thing* [LP]. New York: VP.

Sizzla (2002d). Thank U Mama. On *Da Real Thing* [LP]. New York: VP.

Sizzla (2004a). Jah Works. On *Life* [LP]. London: Greensleeves.

Sizzla (2004b). You World Leaders. On *Jah Knows Best* [LP]. London: Sanctuary.

Sizzla (2004c). Move Up. On *Jah Knows Best* [LP]. London: Sanctuary.

Sizzla (2005a). Be Still. On *Da Real Live Thing* [CD/DVD]. New York: VP.

Sizzla (2005b). Nah Apologize. [7-inch Single]. Kingston: Darkside.

Sizzla (2006). Hot Like Fire. On *Ain't Gonna See Us Fall* [CD]. New York: VP.

Sizzla (2007a). Chant Them Down. On *I-Space* [LP]. London: Greensleeves.

Sizzla (2007b). Only Jah Alone. On *I-Space* [LP]. London: Greensleeves.

Sizzla (2009. Open Up The Doors. On *Ghetto Youth-ology* [CD]. London: Greensleeves.

Sizzla (2013a). Bun Fire. On *Voyage Riddim* [Digital]. Hapilos 21st.

Sizzla (2013b). Show Us The Danger [Digital]. Kingston Elites.

Sizzla (2013c). Black Star Airline. On *Diesel Bounce Riddim* [Digital]. Dynasty Records.

Sizzla (2014). *Mista Savona Presents Sizzla – Born A King* [CD]. San Francisco: Muti Music.

Sugar Roy & Conrad Crystal (2014). Word, Sound And Power. On *The Kings Book* [CD]. Munich: Oneness.

Teflon (2008). *Man A Bobo* [7-inch Single]. Kingston: Chimney.

Teflon (2010). *Uncrowned* [CD]. Canada: Black Ice & Yard A Love.

Teflon (2012). *It's Been A Long Time Coming* [CD]. Canada: Black Ice & Yard A Love.

The Abbyssinians (1976). Satta Massagana. On *Satta Massagana* [LP]. Kingston: Jam Sounds.

The Lost Children of Babylon (2006). *The 911 Report: The Ultimate Conspiracy* [CD]. New York: Babygrande.

The Lost Children of Babylon (2010). *Zeitgeist: The Spirit Of The Age* [CD]. Chamber Music/Soul Kit Records.

The Lost Children of Egypt (2003). Words From The Duat: The Book Of Anubis [CD]. New York: Babygrande.

The Reavers (2005). Warrior. On *Terror Firma* [CD]. New York: Green Streets Entertainment.

TOK (2001). Chi Chi Man. On *My Crew, My Dawgs* [CD]. New York: VP.

Turbulence (2005). I Will Survive. On *Riddim Driven – Lion Paw* [CD]. New York: VP.

Turbulence (2015). Bobo Stepin. [Digital]. Kingston: Dub Dragon.

Walker, S. (1975). Burn Babylon. [7-inch Single]. Kingston: Joe Gibbs Record Globe.

Wu-Tang Clan (1993). C.R.E.A.M. On *Enter The Wu Tang (36 Chambers)*. [LP]. New York: Loud.

Wu-Tang Clan (1997a). Wu-Revolution. On *Wu-Tang Forever* [2LP]. New York: Loud.

Wu-Tang Clan (1997b).Triumph. On *Wu-Tang Forever* [2LP]. New York: Loud.

Wu-Tang Clan (1997c). It's Yourz. On *Wu-Tang Forever* [2LP]. New York: Loud.